5 STEPS TO A

5

500
AP Physics C Questions
to know by test day

Also in the 5 Steps series:
5 Steps to a 5: AP Physics C, 2018

Also in the 500 AP Questions to Know by Test Day series:
5 Steps to a 5: 500 AP Biology Questions to Know by Test Day, Second Edition
5 Steps to a 5: 500 AP Calculus AB/BC Questions to Know by Test Day
5 Steps to a 5: 500 AP Chemistry Questions to Know by Test Day, Second Edition
5 Steps to a 5: 500 AP English Language Questions to Know by Test Day, Second Edition
5 Steps to a 5: 500 AP English Literature Questions to Know by Test Day
5 Steps to a 5: 500 AP Environmental Science Questions to Know by Test Day, Second Edition
5 Steps to a 5: 500 AP European History Questions to Know by Test Day, Second Edition
5 Steps to a 5: 500 AP Human Geography, Second Edition
5 Steps to a 5: 500 AP Macroeconomics Questions to Know by Test Day, Second Edition
5 Steps to a 5: 500 AP Microeconomics Questions to Know by Test Day, Second Edition
5 Steps to a 5: 500 AP Physics 1 Questions to Know by Test Day, Second Edition
5 Steps to a 5: 500 AP Psychology Questions to Know by Test Day, Second Edition
5 Steps to a 5: 500 AP Statistics Questions to Know by Test Day, Second Edition
5 Steps to a 5: 500 AP U.S. Government & Politics Questions to Know by Test Day
5 Steps to a 5: 500 AP U.S. History Questions to Know by Test Day, Second Edition
5 Steps to a 5: 500 AP World History Questions to Know by Test Day, Second Edition

5 STEPS TO A

5

™

500
AP Physics C Questions
to know by test day

Hugh Henderson

Mc
Graw
Hill
Education

New York   Chicago   San Francisco   Athens   London   Madrid
Mexico City   Milan   New Delhi   Singapore   Sydney   Toronto

1 2 3 4 5 6 7 8 9   QFR   21 20 19 18 17

ISBN   978-1-259-86002-7
MHID   1-259-86002-7

e-ISBN 978-1-259-86003-4
e-MHID   1-259-86003-5

McGraw-Hill Education, the McGraw-Hill Education logo, 5 Steps to a 5, and related trade dress are trademarks or registered trademarks of McGraw-Hill Education and/or its affiliates in the United States and other countries and may not be used without written permission. All other trademarks are the property of their respective owners. McGraw-Hill Education is not associated with any product or vendor mentioned in this book.

AP, Advanced Placement Program, and College Board are registered trademarks of the College Board, which was not involved in the production of, and does not endorse, this product.

McGraw-Hill Education products are available at special quantity discounts to use as premiums and sales promotions or for use in corporate training programs. To contact a representative, please visit the Contact Us pages at www.mhprofessional.com.

CONTENTS

INTRODUCTION

Congratulations! You've taken a big step toward AP success by purchasing *5 Steps to a 5: 500 AP Physics C Questions to Know by Test Day*. We are here to help you take the next step and score high on your AP Exam so you can earn college credits and get into the college or university of your choice.

This book gives you 500 AP-style multiple-choice questions that cover all the most essential course material, in addition to short essay questions at the end of each chapter similar to those on the AP exam. Each question has a detailed answer explanation that can be found at the back of the book. These questions will give you valuable independent practice to supplement your regular textbook and the groundwork you are already doing in your AP classroom. This and the other books in this series were written by expert AP teachers who know your exam inside and out and can identify the crucial exam information as well as questions that are most likely to appear on the test.

You might be the kind of student who takes several AP courses and needs to study extra questions a few weeks before the exam for a final review. Or you might be the kind of student who puts off preparing until the last weeks before the exam. No matter what your preparation style is, you will surely benefit from reviewing these 500 questions, which closely parallel the content, format, and degree of difficulty of the questions on the actual AP Exam. These questions and their answer explanations are the ideal last-minute study tool for those final few weeks before the test.

Remember the old saying "Practice makes perfect." If you practice with all the questions and answers in this book, we are certain you will build the skills and confidence needed to do great on the exam. Good luck!

—Editors of McGraw-Hill Education

5 STEPS TO A >5

500
AP Physics C Questions
to know by test day

CHAPTER 1

Kinematics

On all of the questions in this book, you may neglect air resistance and use $g = 10$ m/s^2 unless otherwise noted.

Questions 1–3
A ball of mass 0.5 kg is launched horizontally from the top of a cliff 80 m high with a speed of 20 m/s at time $t = 0$.

1. The horizontal distance x traveled by the ball before striking the ground is

    (A) 20 m
    (B) 40 m
    (C) 80 m
    (D) 160 m
    (E) 320 m

2. Which of the following graphs best represents the vertical speed v_y of the ball from $t = 0$ until just before the ball strikes the ground?

(A) v_y

(B) v_y

(C) v_y

(D) v_y

(E) v_y

3. The speed of the ball just before striking the ground is
(A) 4 m/s
(B) 14 m/s
(C) 20 m/s
(D) 44 m/s
(E) 64 m/s

Questions 4–5

A sprinter starting from rest runs a 100-meter race on a straight track. The sprinter covers the first 10 meters with a constant acceleration in 2 seconds. The sprinter runs the remaining 90 m with the same velocity he had at the end of 2 s.

4. The sprinter's velocity at the end of the first 2 s is

   (A) 5 m/s
   (B) 10 m/s
   (C) 20 m/s
   (D) 40 m/s
   (E) 60 m/s

5. The total time it takes for the sprinter to run the full 100 m is

   (A) 2 s
   (B) 9 s
   (C) 10 s
   (D) 11 s
   (E) 12 s

2 kg

1.2 m

6. A block of mass 2 kg is attached to a string that is wrapped around a pulley of negligible mass and allowed to descend from rest a vertical distance of 1.2 m in a time of 1.5 s. The acceleration of the block is most nearly

   (A) 0.2 m/s²
   (B) 0.6 m/s²
   (C) 1.1 m/s²
   (D) 1.4 m/s²
   (E) 1.5 m/s²

7. A helicopter raises a package with an upward constant speed of 3 m/s. The rope suddenly breaks when the package is 8 meters above the ground. Neglecting air resistance, calculate the speed at which the package strikes the ground.

    (A) 13 m/s
    (B) 26 m/s
    (C) 84 m/s
    (D) 169 m/s
    (E) 202 m/s

8. A ball is attached to a string of length 0.8 m and is swung in a vertical circle. The bottom of the circle is 0.2 m above the floor. If the string breaks at the top of the circle when the speed of the ball is 5 m/s, the horizontal distance the ball travels before striking the floor is

    (A) 0.8 m
    (B) 2.3 m
    (C) 3.0 m
    (D) 5.0 m
    (E) 13.2 m

9. A golf ball is hit from level ground and has a horizontal range of 100 m. The ball leaves the golf club at an angle of 60° to the level ground. At what other angle(s) can the ball be struck at the same initial velocity and still have a range of 100 m?

(A) 30°

(B) 20° and 80°

(C) 10° and 120°

(D) 45° and 135°

(E) There is no other angle other than 60° in which the ball will have a range of 100 m.

10. A small cart is moving with an initial positive velocity of 4.0 m/s on a track of negligible friction when it rolls up the ramp, just makes it over the top, and rolls back down the ramp. The cart then rolls along the level track. Which of the following graphs best represents the velocity vs. time graph for the entire trip?

    (A) v

    (B) v

    (C) v

    (D) v

    (E) v

Questions 11–12. A particle moves on a horizontal surface with a constant acceleration of 6 m/s² in the *x*-direction and 4 m/s² in the *y*-direction. The initial velocity of the particle is 3 m/s in the *x*-direction.

11. The speed of the particle after 4 s is

    (A) 16 m/s
    (B) 27 m/s
    (C) 31 m/s
    (D) 44 m/s
    (E) 985 m/s

12. The displacement of the particle from its initial position is

    (A) 16 m
    (B) 32 m
    (C) 60 m
    (D) 68 m
    (E) 92 m

13. A space explorer throws a tool downward on a planet with an initial velocity of 2.0 m/s from a height of 6 m above the surface. The tool strikes the surface in a time of 2 s. The acceleration due to gravity on the planet is

    (A) 1 m/s²
    (B) 2 m/s²
    (C) 3 m/s²
    (D) 4 m/s²
    (E) 10 m/s²

Questions 14–15

The graph shown represents the motion of a cart rolling along a horizontal track.

14. The time(s) at which the object is at rest is

(A) zero

(B) 8 s and 36 s

(C) 18 s and 40 s

(D) 24 s and 34 s

(E) 40 s and 50 s

15. The time(s) at which the cart changes direction is

(A) zero

(B) 8 s and 36 s

(C) 18 s and 40 s

(D) 24 s and 34 s

(E) 40 s and 50 s

16. A rubber ball is dropped from rest onto a plane angled at 30° to the horizontal floor and bounces off the plane with a horizontal speed v_o. The ball lands on the plane a distance D along the plane, as shown. In terms of v_o, D, and g, the speed of the ball just before striking the plane is

   (A) v_o

   (B) $\left(v_o^2 + 2D\sin\theta g\right)^{\frac{1}{2}}$

   (C) $\left(v_o + \dfrac{D\sin\theta}{g}\right)^{\frac{1}{2}}$

   (D) $\left(v_o^2 + \dfrac{2D\sin\theta}{g}\right)^{\frac{1}{2}}$

   (E) $(2D\sin\theta g)^{\frac{1}{2}}$

17. A projectile is launched from a platform 20 m high above level ground. The projectile is launched with a velocity of 40 m/s at an angle of 60° above the horizontal. The projectile follows a parabolic path and reaches its original height at a horizontal distance of 80 m, but moves past the height of the cliff to strike the ground below. The total time from the launch until it strikes the ground is

   (A) 2 s
   (B) 4 s
   (C) 6 s
   (D) 9 s
   (E) 10 s

Questions 18–19
A stack of coffee filters falls from rest through the air. Due to air resistance, the filters fall with an acceleration proportional to the velocity of fall, that is, $a = -kv$, where k is a positive constant.

18. The velocity of the falling filters as a function of time of fall is
    (A) $-kv^2$
    (B) $-\frac{1}{2}kv^2$
    (C) $-k$
    (D) $\ln (kt)$
    (E) $v_o e^{-kt}$

19. Which of the following best represents the graph of velocity vs. time from $t = 0$ until the filters reach terminal velocity?

    (A)

    (B)

    (C)

    (D)

    (E)

20. A small ball is launched with a speed of 8 m/s at an angle of 30° from the horizontal. A cup is hung so that it is in position to catch the ball when it reaches its maximum height. How far above the floor should the cup be hung to catch the ball?

   (A) 2.4 m
   (B) 1.6 m
   (C) 1.0 m
   (D) 0.8 m
   (E) 0.4 m

Questions 21–22. A car of mass m travels along a straight horizontal road. The car begins with a speed v_o, but accelerates according to the velocity function $v = \left(v_o^2 + \dfrac{Ct^2}{m} \right)$, where t is time.

21. The speed of the car is zero at a time t of

   (A) zero
   (B) $2t$
   (C) $4t$
   (D) $\sqrt{8t}$
   (E) The speed of the car is never zero.

22. The acceleration of the car as a function of time is

   (A) $\left(v_o^2 + \dfrac{Ct^2}{m} \right)$

   (B) $\left(v_o^2 + \dfrac{2Ct}{m} \right)$

   (C) $\left(v_o + \dfrac{2Ct}{m} \right)$

   (D) $\left(\dfrac{2Ct}{m} \right)$

   (E) $\left(\dfrac{2Ct^2}{m} \right)$

Questions 23–24. The graph shown represents the velocity vs. time graphs for two cars, P and Q. Car P begins with a speed v_P, and Car Q begins with a speed v_Q which is twice the velocity of Car P, that is, $v_Q = 2v_P$.

23. Which of the following is true at a time of 10 s?
    (A) The cars occupy the same position.
    (B) Car P is at rest.
    (C) $v_Q > v_P$
    (D) $v_P > v_Q$
    (E) Car Q is ahead of Car P.

24. Which of the following is true at a time of 20 s?
    (A) The cars occupy the same position.
    (B) Car P is at rest.
    (C) $v_Q > v_P$
    (D) $a_P = a_Q$
    (E) Car P is ahead of Car Q.

25. The velocity vs. time graph above represents the motion of a bicycle rider. The displacement of the rider between 0 and 4 h is

(A) +10 km
(B) +20 km
(C) +30 km
(D) +40 km
(E) −10 km

26. A car is initially moving with a positive velocity of 20 m/s when it passes the origin at time $t = 0$. The car continues to move at +20 m/s between $t = 0$ and $t = 2$ s. At $t = 2$ s, the driver presses the brake, giving the car an acceleration of −4 m/s². The displacement of the car at $t = 6$ s is

(A) 40 m
(B) 32 m
(C) 48 m
(D) 64 m
(E) 88 m

27. Which of the following pairs of graphs could show the position vs. time and velocity vs. time graphs for the acceleration vs. time graph shown above? Assume $v = 0$ and $x = 0$ at $t = 0$.

(A)

(B)

(C)

(D)

(E)

28. A small airplane can fly at 200 km/h with no wind. The pilot of the plane would like to fly to a destination 100 km due north of his present position, but there is a crosswind of 50 km/h east. How much time is required for the plane to fly north to its destination?

    (A) less than ½ h
    (B) ½ h
    (C) more than ½ h
    (D) 1 h
    (E) more than 1 h

Graph 1   Graph 2

29. Two velocity vectors v_1 and v_2 each have a magnitude of 10 m/s. Graph 1 shows the velocity v_1 at $t = 0$ s, and then the same object has a velocity v_2 at $t = 2$ s, shown in Graph 2. Which of the following vectors best represents the average acceleration vector that causes the object's velocity to change from v_1 to v_2?

(A)

(B)

(C)

(D)

(E)

30. An object starts from rest at $t = 0$ and position $x = 0$, then moves in a straight line with an acceleration described by the equation $a = 4t^2$ in m/s². What is the position of the object at $t = 3$ s?

    (A) 6 m
    (B) 18 m
    (C) 27 m
    (D) 54 m
    (E) 108 m

31. A ball is dropped from rest from the top of a cliff 80 meters high. At the same time, a rock is thrown horizontally from the top of the same cliff. The rock and ball hit the level ground below a distance of 40 m apart. The horizontal velocity of the rock that was thrown was most nearly

    (A) 5 m/s
    (B) 10 m/s
    (C) 20 m/s
    (D) 40 m/s
    (E) 80 m/s

32. A stone is dropped near the surface of Mars and falls with an acceleration of 3.8 m/s². This means that the

    (A) distance the stone falls increases 3.8 meters for each second of fall
    (B) derivative of the distance fallen with respect to time is 3.8 m/s
    (C) derivative of the velocity with respect to time is 3.8 m/s²
    (D) velocity is constant at 3.8 m/s
    (E) derivative of the acceleration is 3.8 m/s²

33. A 600 kg car accelerates uniformly from rest. After 4 s, it reaches a speed of 24 m/s. During the 4 s, the car has traveled a distance of

(A) 12 m
(B) 24 m
(C) 36 m
(D) 48 m
(E) 96 m

34. A passenger on a train moving horizontally at a constant speed relative to the ground drops a ball from his window. A stationary observer on the ground sees the ball falling with a speed v_1 at an angle to the vertical at the instant it is dropped from the train window, but the ball appears to be falling vertically with a speed v_2 at the same instant as viewed by the train passenger. What is the speed (magnitude of velocity) of the train relative to the ground after the ball is dropped? Neglect air resistance.

(A) $v_1 + v_2$
(B) $v_1 - v_2$
(C) $v_1^2 + v_2^2$
(D) $v_1^2 - v_2^2$
(E) $\sqrt{v_1^2 - v_2^2}$

35. A ball is hit straight up into the air with an upward positive velocity. Which of the following describes the velocity and acceleration of the ball at the instant it reaches the top of its flight?

	Velocity	Acceleration
(A)	0	0
(B)	0	g
(C)	$2 v_o$	g
(D)	$\frac{1}{2} v_o$	0
(E)	0	$\frac{1}{2} g$

36. A toy dart gun fires a dart at an angle of 45° to the horizontal and the dart reaches a maximum height of 1 meter. If the dart were fired straight up into the air along the vertical, the dart would reach a height of

(A) 1 m

(B) 2 m

(C) 3 m

(D) 4 m

(E) 5 m

Questions 37–38

A projectile is launched at the angle and follows the trajectory shown below.

37. Which of the following indicates the direction of the velocity at point A?

(A) ↑

(B) ←

(C) →

(D) ↖

(E) ↓

38. Which of the following indicates the direction of the acceleration at point B?

(A) ↑

(B) ←

(C) →

(D) ↖

(E) ↓

39. The graph above shows the displacement as a function of time for a car moving in a straight line. Which of the following graphs shows the velocity vs. time graph for the same time intervals?

(A)

(B)

(C)

(D)

(E)

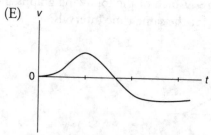

Questions 40–41

40. An object is released from rest and falls through a resistive medium. The resistance causes the velocity of the object to change according to the equation $v = 16t - \frac{1}{2}\,t^4$, where v is in m/s and time is in s. Which of the following is a possible equation for the acceleration of the object as a function of time?

(A) $16 - 2t^2$

(B) $16 - 2t^3$

(C) $16 - 2t$

(D) $8t^3 - 2t^2$

(E) $32t^3 - 2t^5$

41. What is the terminal velocity of the object as it falls?

(A) 5 m/s

(B) 10 m/s

(C) 24 m/s

(D) 32 m/s

(E) The object never reaches a terminal velocity.

42. A student jumps off a cliff with an initial horizontal velocity v and lands in a lake below at a distance of x from the base of the cliff. In terms of his initial velocity v, how fast would he have had to jump to land a distance $2x$ from the base of the cliff?

   (A) $\sqrt{2}v$
   (B) $2v$
   (C) $4v$
   (D) $8v$
   (E) $16v$

43. An astronaut drops a hammer on a moon with no atmosphere. The hammer falls a distance of 2 meters in the first second. What is the acceleration due to gravity on this moon?

   (A) 1 m/s^2
   (B) 2 m/s^2
   (C) 3 m/s^2
   (D) 4 m/s^2
   (E) 8 m/s^2

44. A car travels 300 m in 60 s, then travels 200 m in 30 s. The average speed of the car is

   (A) 5.6 m/s
   (B) 5.0 m/s
   (C) 3.0 m/s
   (D) 2.3 m/s
   (E) 12.0 m/s

45. The motion of an object is represented by the acceleration vs. time graph above. Which of the following statements is true about the motion of the object?

   (A) The object returns to its original position.
   (B) The velocity of the object is zero at a time of 2 s.
   (C) The velocity of the object is zero at a time of 4 s.
   (D) The displacement of the object is zero at a time of 4 s.
   (E) The acceleration of the object is zero at a time of 2 s.

Free Response

The acceleration vs. time graph shows the motion of an elevator during a 20-second time interval. The elevator starts from rest at time $t = 0$.

46. Determine the instantaneous velocity of the elevator at the end of 10 s.

47. Determine the displacement of the elevator after 5 s.

48. On the axes below, sketch the graph that represents the velocity vs. time graph for the elevator for the 20-second time interval.

Questions 49–50. A particle follows a parabolic path with the equation $y = 2x^2$ as shown. The x-component of the particle's velocity v_x as a function of time t is 6, that is, the horizontal displacement is $x = 6t$.

49. Determine the y-component of the particle's velocity v_y as a function of time.

50. On the diagram below, sketch arrows to represent the horizontal and vertical components of the particle's acceleration at point P.

Dynamics: Newton's Laws of Motion

On all of the questions in this book, you may neglect air resistance and use $g = 10$ m/s^2 unless otherwise noted.

51. Which of the following involves a net force?

   I. A ball on the end of a string travels in circular motion.
   II. A space probe travels with a constant velocity in a straight line between planets.
   III. An object has a constant horizontal velocity, but a decreasing vertical velocity.

   (A) I only
   (B) I and II only
   (C) II and III only
   (D) I and III only
   (E) I, II, and III

52. A small moving block collides with a large block at rest. Which of the following is true of the forces the blocks apply to each other?

   (A) The small block exerts twice the force on the large block compared to the force the large block exerts on the small block.
   (B) The small block exerts half the force on the large block compared to the force the large block exerts on the small block.
   (C) The small block exerts exactly the same amount of force on the large block that the large block exerts on the small block.
   (D) The large block exerts a force on the small block, but the small block does not exert a force on the large block.
   (E) The small block exerts a force on the large block, but the large block does not exert a force on the small block.

53. Which of the following *position vs. time* graphs shows an example of the law of inertia?

(A)

(B)

(C)

(D)

(E)

Questions 54–55. Two blocks, 4.0 kg and 2.0 kg, are connected by a string. An applied force *F* of magnitude 18 N pulls the blocks to the left.

54. The acceleration of the 4.0 kg block is

(A) 2.0 m/s²
(B) 3.0 m/s²
(C) 4.0 m/s²
(D) 4.5 m/s²
(E) 6.0 m/s²

55. The tension in the string between the blocks is

(A) 4.0 N
(B) 6.0 N
(C) 12 N
(D) 16 N
(E) 18 N

Questions 56–57. A system consists of two blocks having masses of 2 kg and 1 kg. The blocks are connected by a string of negligible mass and hung over a light pulley, and then released from rest.

56. The acceleration of the 2 kg block is most nearly

(A) 2/9 g
(B) 1/3 g
(C) 1/2 g
(D) 2/3 g
(E) g

57. The speed of the 2 kg block after it has descended a distance D is most nearly

    (A) $\sqrt{\dfrac{4D}{3}}$

    (B) $\sqrt{\dfrac{2D}{3}}$

    (C) $\sqrt{\dfrac{D}{3}}$

    (D) $\sqrt{\dfrac{D}{2}}$

    (E) $\sqrt{\dfrac{4D}{6}}$

Questions 58–59. A weight of magnitude W is suspended in equilibrium by two cords, one horizontal and one slanted at an angle of 60° from the horizontal, as shown.

58. Which of the following statements is true?

    (A) The tension in the horizontal cord must be greater than the tension in the slanted cord.
    (B) The tension in the slanted cord must be greater than the tension in the horizontal cord.
    (C) The tension is the same in both cords.
    (D) The tension in the horizontal cord equals the weight W.
    (E) The tension in the slanted cord equals the weight W.

59. The tension in the horizontal cord is

(A) equal to the tension in the slanted cord
(B) one-third as much as the tension in the slanted cord
(C) one-half as much as the tension in the slanted cord
(D) twice as much as the tension in the slanted cord
(E) three times as much as the tension in the slanted cord

Questions 60–61. An object of mass m moves along a straight line with a speed described by the equation $v = c + bt^3$.

60. The initial velocity of the mass is

(A) c
(B) $ct + bt^3$
(C) $ct + bt^4$
(D) bt^2
(E) bt

61. The net force acting on the mass at time T is

(A) $3mbT$
(B) $3mbT^2$
(C) $3mbT^3$
(D) $mc + 2mbT^2$
(E) $mc^2 + 4mbT^4$

62. A wooden block slides down a frictionless inclined plane a distance of 1 meter along the plane during the first second. The distance traveled along the plane by the block during the time between 1 s and 2 s is

(A) 2 m
(B) 3 m
(C) 4 m
(D) 6 m
(E) 8 m

63. A mass located at point P follows a parabolic path. Which of the following diagrams indicates a possible combination of the net force **F** acting on the mass, the velocity **v**, and acceleration **a** of the mass at point P?

(A)

(B)

(C)

(D)

(E)

Questions 64–65. Three blocks of mass 3 kg, 2 kg, and 1 kg are pushed along a horizontal frictionless plane by a force of 24 N to the right, as shown.

64. The acceleration of the 2 kg block is

    (A) 144 m/s^2
    (B) 72 m/s^2
    (C) 12 m/s^2
    (D) 6 m/s^2
    (E) 4 m/s^2

65. The force that the 2 kg block exerts on the 1 kg block is

    (A) 2 N
    (B) 4 N
    (C) 6 N
    (D) 24 N
    (E) 144 N

66. A hockey puck slides along horizontal ice with a velocity v_1 when it is struck by a hockey stick, changing its direction, as shown. After the puck is struck, it has a velocity v_2, which is greater than v_1. Which of the following vectors best represents the direction the force of the hockey stick acted on the puck?

    (A) ↑
    (B) ←
    (C) →
    (D) ↖
    (E) ↗

67. A block of mass 4 kg slides down a rough incline with a constant speed. The angle the incline makes with the horizontal is 30°. The coefficient of friction acting between the block and incline is most nearly

    (A) 0.1
    (B) 0.2
    (C) 0.3
    (D) 0.4
    (E) 0.6

68. An object of mass 3 kg moves along a straight line on the y-axis according to the equation $y = 8t - 4t^2 + t^3$, where y is in meters and t is in seconds. The net force acting on the mass is zero at a time of

    (A) ¾ s
    (B) 4/3 s
    (C) 8/3 s
    (D) 2 s
    (E) 4 s

69. A ball is thrown straight up into the air, encountering air resistance as it rises. What forces, if any, act on the ball as it rises?

    (A) A decreasing gravitational force and an increasing force of air resistance
    (B) An increasing gravitational force and an increasing force of air resistance
    (C) A decreasing gravitational force and a decreasing force of air resistance
    (D) A constant gravitational force and an increasing force of air resistance
    (E) A constant gravitational force and a decreasing force of air resistance

Questions 70–71

An 800 kg elevator is supported by a vertical cable.

70. The cable has a tension of 10,000 N as it accelerates the elevator upward from rest to a height of 10 m. The acceleration of the elevator is most nearly

(A) 1.0 m/s^2
(B) 2.0 m/s^2
(C) 2.5 m/s^2
(D) 3.5 m/s^2
(E) 4.0 m/s^2

71. The elevator passes the 10 m height on the way up, stops, then begins its descent downward, having an initial velocity as it passes the 10 m height on the way down. If the tension in the cable is now 6000 N, and it comes to rest just before reaching the ground, the initial velocity at the 10 m height must have been most nearly

(A) 5.0 m/s
(B) 7.0 m/s
(C) 29.5 m/s
(D) 12.5 m/s
(E) 16.0 m/s

72. A weight W is hung from two threads, A and B, as shown above. The magnitudes of the tensions in each string are F_A and F_B, respectively. Which of the following describes the relationship between F_A, F_B, and W?

    (A) $F_A = F_B = W$
    (B) $F_A = F_B$
    (C) $F_A < F_B$
    (D) $F_A > F_B$
    (E) $F_A + F_B = W$

Questions 73–74
A 1 kg block is sliding up a rough 30° incline and is slowing down with an acceleration of −6 m/s². The mass has a weight **W**, and encounters a frictional force **f** and a normal force **N**.

73. Which of the following free body diagrams best represents the forces acting on the block as it slides up the plane?

(A)

(B)

(C)

(D)

(E)

74. The magnitude of the frictional force f between the block and the plane is most nearly

    (A) 1 N
    (B) 2 N
    (C) 3 N
    (D) 4 N
    (E) 5 N

75. A force gives an 8 kg mass an acceleration of 3 m/s². The same force will give a 12 kg mass an acceleration of

    (A) 1 m/s²
    (B) 2 m/s²
    (C) 3 m/s²
    (D) 4 m/s²
    (E) 6 m/s²

4 kg   2 kg

76. Two blocks are pulled by a force of magnitude F along a level surface with negligible friction as shown. The tension in the string between the blocks is

    (A) ¼ F
    (B) ½ F
    (C) 1/3 F
    (D) F
    (E) 2F

77. A force of magnitude F pulls up at an angle θ to the horizontal on a block of mass m. The mass remains in contact with the level floor and the coefficient of friction between the block and the floor is μ. The frictional force between the floor and the block is

   (A) μmg
   (B) $\mu(mg - F\sin\theta)$
   (C) $\mu(mg + F\sin\theta)$
   (D) $\mu(mg - F\cos\theta)$
   (E) $\mu(mg + F\cos\theta)$

78. A block weighing 60 N hangs from three ropes as shown. Which of the following statements is true?

   (A) Each rope has a tension of 60 N.
   (B) The tension in each rope is higher in the lower part than in the upper part of the rope.
   (C) The tension in each rope is higher in the upper part than in the lower part of the rope.
   (D) The rope in the center has a higher tension than the other two ropes.
   (E) Each rope has a tension of 20 N.

79. A stone falls through the air toward the Earth's surface. The resistive force the air applies to the stone as it falls is given by the equation $F = cv$, where c is a positive constant and v is the speed of the stone. The acceleration of the ball is given by the equation

(A) $c - g$

(B) gcv/m

(C) $g + cv$

(D) $g - cv/m$

(E) cv/m

80. A block of mass $4m$ can move without friction on a horizontal surface. Another block of mass m is attached to the larger block by a string that is passed over a light pulley. The acceleration of the system is

(A) $1/5\ g$

(B) $\frac{1}{2}\ g$

(C) $2/3\ g$

(D) g

(E) $5g$

81. The block of mass $4m$ in the previous question now moves on a rough surface. The frictional force between the surface and the larger block is equal to $\frac{1}{2}\ mg$. The acceleration of the system is now

(A) $1/16\ g$

(B) $1/10\ g$

(C) $\frac{1}{4}\ g$

(D) $\frac{1}{2}\ g$

(E) g

Questions 82–83. A 10 N block sits atop an inclined plane in the shape of a right triangle of sides 3 m, 4 m, and 5 m, as shown. The block is allowed to slide down the plane with negligible friction.

82. The acceleration of the block is most nearly

   (A) 2 m/s^2
   (B) 4 m/s^2
   (C) 6 m/s^2
   (D) 10 m/s^2
   (E) 12 m/s^2

83. The normal force exerted on the block by the plane is most nearly

   (A) 2 N
   (B) 4 N
   (C) 6 N
   (D) 8 N
   (E) 10 N

84. A projectile is launched at an angle and follows a parabolic path near the Earth's surface. Which of the following best indicates the net force acting on the projectile at the top of its path, if any?

   (A) ↑
   (B) ←
   (C) →
   (D) ↖
   (E) ↓

85. Three strings are attached to a ring in the center of a force table. The top view of the force table is shown. For the ring to remain in the center of the table, which of the following must be true?

    (A) The vector sum of the three forces must equal zero.
    (B) The lengths of the strings must be equal.
    (C) The strings must form an angle of 90° relative to each other.
    (D) The magnitudes of two of the tensions in the strings must equal the tension in the third string.
    (E) The tension in each string must be equal to each other.

Questions 86–87. The position of a 2 kg object is described by the equation $x = 2t^2 - 3t^3$, where x is in meters and t is in seconds.

86. The net force acting on the object at a time of 1 s is

    (A) −4 N
    (B) −8 N
    (C) −14 N
    (D) −20 N
    (E) −24 N

87. The net force acting on the object is positive from $t = 0$ until a time of

    (A) 0.11 s
    (B) 0.22 s
    (C) 0.44 s
    (D) 0.67 s
    (E) 1.0 s

Questions 88–89. A particle of mass 0.5 kg moves in two dimensions according to the velocity equation $v = 4t^2\,\mathbf{i} + 6t^4\,\mathbf{j}$, where speed is in m/s and time is in s.

88. The acceleration of the particle at time $t = 1$ s in m/s^2 is

   (A) $a = 8\,\mathbf{i} + 24\,\mathbf{j}$
   (B) $a = 24\,\mathbf{i} + 8\,\mathbf{j}$
   (C) $a = 8\,\mathbf{i} + 48\,\mathbf{j}$
   (D) $a = 4\,\mathbf{i} + 6\,\mathbf{j}$
   (E) $a = 2\,\mathbf{i} + 8\,\mathbf{j}$

89. The magnitude of the net force acting on the particle at a time of 2 s is most nearly

   (A) 36 N
   (B) 64 N
   (C) 72 N
   (D) 84 N
   (E) 104 N

90. A constant force acts on a particle in such a way that the direction of the force is always perpendicular to its velocity. Which of the following is true of the particle's motion?

   (A) The acceleration of the particle is increasing
   (B) The acceleration of the particle is decreasing.
   (C) The speed of the particle is increasing.
   (D) The speed of the particle is constant.
   (E) The speed of the particle is decreasing.

91. A coffee filter is released from rest at a height of 3 meters above the floor. Which of the following graphs best describes the speed of the falling coffee filter as a function of time?

(A)

(B)

(C)

(D)

(E)

Questions 92–93. A block of mass 2 kg rests on top of a larger block of mass 4 kg. The larger block slides without friction on a table, but the surface between the two blocks is not frictionless. The coefficient of friction between the two blocks is 0.2. A horizontal force **F** is applied to the 4 kg mass.

92. What is the maximum force that can be applied such that there is no relative motion between the two blocks?

    (A) zero
    (B) 1 N
    (C) 2 N
    (D) 4 N
    (E) 12 N

93. What is the acceleration of the 2 kg block **relative to the 4 kg block** if a force is applied to the 4 kg block that causes the 4 kg block to accelerate at 3 m/s^2 to the right?

    (A) 1 m/s^2 to the right
    (B) 1 m/s^2 to the left
    (C) 2 m/s^2 to the right
    (D) 2 m/s^2 to the left
    (E) zero

Free Response

Questions 94–97. Three masses are connected by two strings as shown. One of the strings is passed over a pulley of negligible mass and friction. The pulley is attached to a stand that rests on a table. The smallest mass is m, the other two masses each have a mass of $2m$, and the mass of the stand is $4m$.

94. If the small mass m is removed, the other two masses hang in equilibrium. Determine the normal force the table exerts on the stand when the system is in equilibrium.

95. The small mass m is once again hung below one of the masses of mass $2m$. Determine the acceleration of the system.

96. Determine the tension in the string between the block of mass $2m$ and the attached block of mass m while the system is accelerating.

97. While the system is accelerating, is the normal force exerted by the table on the stand greater than, equal to, or less than $8mg$? Justify your answer.

_____ greater than $8mg$ _____ equal to $8mg$ _____ less than $8mg$

Questions 98–100. Two blocks weighing 10 N each are connected by a light string that is passed over a light pulley. One of the blocks rests on an inclined plane at an angle of 37° to the horizontal. The friction between the inclined plane and the block is such that the system remains at rest. The length of the ramp is 5 m.

98. Determine the tension in the string while the system is at rest.

99. Determine the frictional force between the block and the inclined plane while the system is at rest.

100. If the string is suddenly cut, what is the speed of the block when it reaches the bottom of the plane?

CHAPTER 3

Work, Energy, Power, and Conservation of Energy

On all of the questions in this book, you may neglect air resistance and use $g = 10 \text{ m/s}^2$ unless otherwise noted.

Questions 101–102. The graph shown represents a force F acting on an object vs. its displacement x.

101. The work done on the object between 0 and 4 meters is

(A) 2 J
(B) 4 J
(C) 6 J
(D) −2 J
(E) −6 J

102. The change in kinetic energy of the object from 0 m to 5 m is

(A) 4 J
(B) 5 J
(C) 5.5 J
(D) −5.5 J
(E) −6 J

103. An object of weight W is lifted at a constant velocity v to a height D in a time t. The power the lifting force supplies is represented by the equation

(A) WD/t
(B) Wt/D
(C) WDt
(D) W/Dt
(E) zero

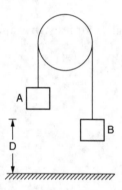

Questions 104–105. Two blocks of mass m_A and m_B are connected by a string that passes over a light pulley. The mass of A is larger than the mass of B.

104. The change in potential energy of the system just before block A reaches the floor is

(A) $(m_A + m_B)gD$
(B) $m_A gD$
(C) $m_B gD$
(D) $(m_A - m_B)gD$
(E) zero

105. The speed of mass A just before reaching the floor is

(A) $\sqrt{\dfrac{(m_A - m_B)}{(m_A + m_B)} gD}$

(B) $\sqrt{\dfrac{(m_A + m_B)}{(m_A - m_B)} gD}$

(C) $\sqrt{\dfrac{(m_A)}{(m_A + m_B)} gD}$

(D) $\sqrt{\dfrac{(m_B)}{(m_A + m_B)} gD}$

(E) $\sqrt{\dfrac{(m_A)}{(m_B)} gD}$

106. Which of the following force F vs. displacement x graphs below will cause the **least** change in kinetic energy of the object on which the force acts? All graphs are drawn to the same scale.

(A)

(B)

(C)

(D)

(E) F

107. A particle of mass m moves according to the displacement equation $x = 2t^{5/2}$. The kinetic energy of the particle as a function of time is

(A) $10mt^{5/2}$
(B) $10mt^{3/2}$
(C) $5/2mt^3$
(D) $5mt^2$
(E) $2mt^{3/2}$

108. A 1 kg ball is thrown vertically downward from a 50-meter-high tower with an initial speed of 4 m/s. Just before striking the ground, the speed of the ball is 20 m/s. The energy lost to air friction is most nearly

(A) 101 J
(B) 210 J
(C) 308 J
(D) 406 J
(E) 508 J

Questions 109–110. A 2 kg projectile is launched with a speed of 20 m/s from horizontal ground at an angle of 37° to the horizontal as shown. Point P is at the top of the path, and point Q is at the end of the path, just before the projectile again reaches the ground.

109. The kinetic energy of the projectile at point P is

(A) 108 J
(B) 225 J
(C) 256 J
(D) 400 J
(E) 525 J

110. The kinetic energy of the projectile at point Q is

(A) 108 J
(B) 225 J
(C) 256 J
(D) 400 J
(E) 525 J

111. A pendulum of mass *m* swings from a vertical angle of 30° as shown. The length of the pendulum is *L*. If the pendulum is released from rest, the speed of the pendulum at the bottom of the swing is

(A) $2gL$
(B) gL
(C) $\sqrt{gL}$
(D) $\sqrt{2gL(L-\cos30°)}$
(E) ½ $gL \cos30°$

112. A 10 N weight is lifted by applying a 15 N upward force. The change in kinetic energy of the weight during this time is equal to the

(A) change in potential energy during this time
(B) the work done by the 10 N weight only
(C) the work done by the 15 N force only
(D) the work done by the 5 N net force
(E) the work done by the algebraic sum of the forces (25 N)

Questions 113–114. A 5 kg object moves along the x-axis with a potential energy function $U = 4x^2 - 2x + 3$, where x is in meters and U is in joules.

113. The potential energy of the object at the origin $(x = 0)$ is

(A) zero
(B) 2 J
(C) 3 J
(D) 6 J
(E) 8 J

114. The magnitude of the force acting on the object at $x = \frac{1}{4}$ m is

(A) zero
(B) 2 N
(C) 4 N
(D) 8 N
(E) 16 N

115. A ball is thrown upward with an initial velocity. At a height of 5 m above the ground, the ball has a potential energy of 30 J relative to the ground. At this height, the ball has a kinetic energy of 20 J. Neglecting air resistance, the maximum height the ball will reach is most nearly

(A) 6 m
(B) 8 m
(C) 10 m
(D) 12 m
(E) 20 m

116. A constant positive force supplies an average power of 6 watts to an object during a certain amount of time. The object has an average velocity of +3 m/s during this time interval. The magnitude of the force is

(A) 2 N
(B) 3 N
(C) 4 N
(D) 6 N
(E) 12 N

Questions 117–118. A 100 kg barbell is lifted at a constant speed by a weightlifter to a height of 2 m in a time of 2 s.

117. The work done by the weightlifter against gravity is

(A) zero
(B) 100 J
(C) 1000 J
(D) 2000 J
(E) 4000 J

118. The power supplied by the weightlifter is

(A) zero
(B) 100 W
(C) 1000 W
(D) 2000 W
(E) 4000 W

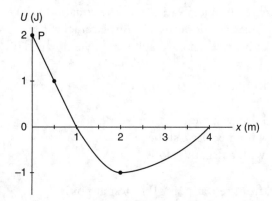

Questions 119–120 refer to the potential energy U vs. displacement x graph shown for a particle moving in one dimension. The force acting on the particle is conservative. The graph begins at point P. The kinetic energy of the particle at position $x = 2$ is 3.0 J. The graph is represented by a straight, diagonal line between $x = 3$ and $x = 4$.

119. The magnitude of the force acting on the particle between $x = 3$ and $x = 4$ is

(A) zero
(B) constant
(C) increasing
(D) decreasing
(E) equal to the weight of the particle

120. Which of the following statements is true of the particle?

(A) The particle is at rest at $x = 2$.

(B) The total energy of the particle at $x = 2$ is +2 J.

(C) The particle has enough energy to reach $x = 1$.

(D) The particle does not have enough energy to reach $x = 3$.

(E) The particle does not have enough energy to reach point P.

121. The force acting on an object varies with the equation $F(x) = -3x^2 - 2x - 4$, where force is in newtons and displacement is in meters. The potential energy at $x = 2$ m is

(A) zero

(B) 20 J

(C) 40 J

(D) −20 J

(E) −40 J

122. The potential energy of an object varies with the equation $U(x) = 2x^2 + x - 6$, where force is in newtons and displacement is in meters. A force F vs. displacement x graph would yield which of the following?

(A) A straight, horizontal line

(B) A parabola

(C) An exponential decay curve

(D) A straight line with a positive slope

(E) A straight line with a negative slope

123. An object is moved from rest at point P to rest at point Q in a gravitational field. The net work against the gravitational field depends on the

(A) mass of the object and the positions of P and Q

(B) mass of the object only

(C) positions of P and Q only

(D) length moved between points P and Q

(E) coefficient of friction

Questions 124–125. A force is applied to a block of mass m at a downward angle of θ to the vertical as shown. The block moves with a constant speed across a rough floor for a distance x.

124. The work done by the applied force on the block is

(A) $Fx\sin\theta$
(B) $Fx\cos\theta$
(C) $Fmx\sin\theta$
(D) $Fmx\cos\theta$
(E) zero

125. The coefficient of friction between the block and the floor is

(A) $\dfrac{F}{mg}$

(B) $\dfrac{F\cos\theta}{mg}$

(C) $\dfrac{F\cos\theta}{F\sin\theta + mg}$

(D) $\dfrac{F\sin\theta}{F\cos\theta + mg}$

(E) $\dfrac{F\cos\theta}{F\sin\theta}$

126. An electron travels in a circle around a hydrogen nucleus at a very high speed. The work done by the electrostatic force acting on the electron after one complete revolution is

(A) zero
(B) positive
(C) negative
(D) equal to the kinetic energy of the electron
(E) equal to the potential energy of the electron

Questions 127–128. The potential energy curve shown refers to a particle having a mass m. The particle is released from rest at the position x_0.

127. The kinetic energy of the particle at position $3x_0$ is

(A) zero

(B) $2U_0$

(C) $3U_0$

(D) $4U_0$

(E) $-2U_0$

128. The speed of the particle at position $3x_0$ is

(A) zero

(B) $\sqrt{\dfrac{U_0}{2m}}$

(C) $\sqrt{\dfrac{U_0}{m}}$

(D) $\sqrt{\dfrac{2U_0}{m}}$

(E) $\sqrt{\dfrac{4U_0}{m}}$

129. A 2.0 m pendulum swings freely with a small amplitude. At its maximum displacement from the vertical, the total energy of the pendulum is 20 J. What is the kinetic energy of the pendulum when its potential energy is 10 J?

(A) zero

(B) 5 J

(C) 10 J

(D) 15 J

(E) 20 J

130. A block slides down a smooth incline from a vertical height *h* so that the work done by gravity is 100 J. The block is then placed at the bottom of the incline and given an initial velocity so that it rises to the same height *h* before coming to rest. The work done by gravity as the block slides up the plane to a height *h* is

(A) 100 J
(B) zero
(C) −100 J
(D) −200 J
(E) The work done by gravity cannot be determined without knowing the mass of the block and the distance it slides along the plane.

Questions 131–132. A 5 kg cannonball is fired with a horizontal velocity from a height of 45 m above level ground below. The cannonball strikes a target on the ground a horizontal distance of 60 m away.

131. The initial horizontal velocity of the cannonball at the instant it was fired is

(A) 5 m/s
(B) 10 m/s
(C) 15 m/s
(D) 20 m/s
(E) 25 m/s

132. The speed of the cannonball just before striking the ground is most nearly

(A) 12 m/s
(B) 21 m/s
(C) 36 m/s
(D) 45 m/s
(E) 90 m/s

Questions 133–134. A ball is thrown from level ground with a velocity at an angle θ above the horizontal so that it follows a parabolic path.

133. Which of the graphs below best represents the kinetic energy of the ball as a function of time until it again reaches the ground?

(A)

(B)

(C)

(D)

(E)

134. Which of the graphs below best represents the potential energy of the ball as a function of time until it again reaches the ground?

(A)

(B)

(C)

(D)

(E)

Questions 135–136. A small block rests on the top of a smooth sphere of radius R when it is given a light tap so that it just begins sliding on the sphere. When the block reaches the angle θ, it loses contact with the surface of the sphere.

135. The kinetic energy of the block as it leaves the surface of the sphere is

(A) mgR

(B) $mgR\cos\theta$

(C) $mgR\sin\theta$

(D) $mg(R - R\cos\theta)$

(E) $mg(R - R\sin\theta)$

136. The speed of the block as it leaves the surface of the sphere is

(A) $\sqrt{\dfrac{2g}{m}}$

(B) $\sqrt{\dfrac{2gR}{m}}$

(C) $\sqrt{2gR\cos\theta}$

(D) $\sqrt{2g(R - R\cos\theta)}$

(E) $\sqrt{2g(R - R\sin\theta)}$

137. A small ball starts from rest and rolls down a quarter-circle ramp of radius R. The speed of the ball at the point halfway down the ramp is most nearly

    (A) gR
    (B) $2gR$
    (C) $\sqrt{gR\sin 45°}$
    (D) $\sqrt{2gR\sin 45°}$
    (E) The speed cannot be determined without knowing the mass of the ball.

138. A machine can lift large weights according to the power equation $P(t) = 4t^3 + 3t^2 - 2$, where power is in watts and time is in seconds. The energy expended by the machine from $t = 0$ to $t = 10$ s is

    (A) 1260 J
    (B) 3630 J
    (C) 9240 J
    (D) 10,080 J
    (E) 18,150 J

139. A power company charges its customers 15¢ per kilowatt-hour. A kilowatt-hour is a unit of

    (A) power
    (B) energy
    (C) electricity
    (D) current
    (E) voltage

140. A boy pushes a crate of mass M across a level floor with a constant speed v. The coefficient of friction between the crate and the floor is μ. What is the rate at which the boy does work on the crate?

 (A) μmg
 (B) mgv
 (C) μmgv
 (D) $\mu mg/v$
 (E) $\mu v/mg$

141. A ballistic pendulum consists of a dart that is launched into a block of wood hanging as a pendulum of length L as shown. When the dart enters the block of wood at point P, the dart and block (total mass m) have a speed v_o and the system is raised to a height h. At this height, the angle of swing is θ. Which of the following is the correct expression for the speed v_o in terms of the other given quantities?

 (A) $\sqrt{\dfrac{2g}{m}}$

 (B) $\sqrt{\dfrac{2gL}{m}}$

 (C) $\sqrt{2gL\cos\theta}$

 (D) $\sqrt{2g(L - L\cos\theta)}$

 (E) $\sqrt{2g(L - L\sin\theta)}$

142. A block slides down a smooth quarter-circle ramp of radius r, then onto a rough flat surface at the bottom of the ramp. The friction on the horizontal surface causes the block to come to rest in a distance d. The work done by the frictional force on the horizontal surface is

(A) mgr

(B) $\sqrt{mgr}$

(C) $2mgr\cos\theta$

(D) $2mg(r - r\cos\theta)$

(E) $2mg(r - r\sin\theta)$

Questions 143–144. A 1 kg rubber ball is thrown vertically downward and strikes the floor with a speed of 12 m/s, bounces off the floor, and then rises to a height of 4 m.

143. The speed of the ball immediately after it strikes the floor is most nearly

(A) 4 m/s

(B) 9 m/s

(C) 12 m/s

(D) 16 m/s

(E) 80 m/s

144. The fraction of the ball's kinetic energy that is apparently lost during the bounce is

(A) 0.25

(B) 0.44

(C) 0.55

(D) 0.70

(E) 0.89

Free Response

Questions 145–147. A girl pushes a 20 kg box across a rough horizontal floor at a constant speed of 2.0 m/s for a distance of 6.0 m. The coefficient of friction between the box and the floor is 0.4.

145. Determine the force the girl must apply over this distance.

146. Determine the work done by the girl over this distance.

147. Determine the power supplied by the girl.

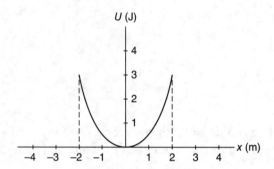

Questions 148–150. A 2.0 kg object's potential energy $U(x)$ is described by the graph shown. The object has a total energy of 3.0 J.

148. What is the farthest the object can move along the x-axis?

149. What is the object's kinetic energy when its displacement is −1 m?

150. What is the object's speed at $x = 0$?

CHAPTER 4

Impulse, Linear Momentum, and Conservation of Linear Momentum

On all of the questions in this book, you may neglect air resistance and use $g = 10 \text{ m/s}^2$ unless otherwise noted.

151. A toy train car of mass 3.0 kg rolls to the left at 2 m/s and collides with a 4.0 kg train car rolling to the right at 1 m/s. The two cars stick together. The velocity of the cars after the collision is

(A) 2/7 m/s to the left
(B) 2/7 m/s to the right
(C) 4/7 m/s to the left
(D) 4/7 m/s to the right
(E) 9/7 m/s to the right

152. Two steel balls, one of mass m and the other of mass $2m$, collide and rebound in a perfectly elastic collision. Which of the following is conserved in this elastic collision?

(A) velocity only
(B) momentum only
(C) momentum and kinetic energy only
(D) momentum, velocity, and kinetic energy
(E) kinetic energy only

Questions 153–154. A force acts on a 2.0 kg mass during a time interval as shown in the graph.

153. The impulse given to the mass from $t = 0$ to $t = 6$ s is

(A) 4 N s
(B) 8 N s
(C) 12 N s
(D) 16 N s
(E) 24 N s

154. If the initial speed of the mass is 2 m/s at $t = 0$, what is its speed at the end of 6 s?

(A) 4 m/s
(B) 6 m/s
(C) 8 m/s
(D) 10 m/s
(E) 16 m/s

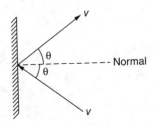

155. A rubber ball of mass m strikes a wall with a speed v at an angle θ below the normal line and rebounds from the wall at the same speed and angle above the normal line as shown. The change in momentum of the ball is

(A) mv
(B) $2mv$
(C) $mv\cos\theta$
(D) $2mv\cos\theta$
(E) zero

156. Two blocks are connected by a compressed spring and rest on a frictionless surface. The blocks are released from rest and pushed apart by the compressed spring. If one mass is twice the mass of the other, which of the following is the same for both blocks?

(A) magnitude of momentum
(B) acceleration
(C) speed
(D) kinetic energy
(E) potential energy

157. A 1000 kg railroad car is rolling without friction on a horizontal track at a speed of 3.0 m/s. Sand is poured into the open top of the car for a time of 5.0 s. The speed of the car after 5.0 s is 1.0 m/s. The mass of the sand added to the car at the end of 5.0 s is
    (A) 500 kg
    (B) 1000 kg
    (C) 2000 kg
    (D) 3000 kg
    (E) 3500 kg

158. Two billiard balls are rolling to the right on a table as shown. The 0.4 kg ball is moving faster than the 0.2 kg ball, so it catches up and strikes it from behind at a slight angle. Immediately after the collision, the y-component of the 0.4 kg ball is 2 m/s downward. The y-component of the velocity of the 0.2 kg ball must be
    (A) 1 m/s upward
    (B) 2 m/s upward
    (C) 1 m/s downward
    (D) 2 m/s downward
    (E) 4 m/s upward

Questions 159–160. Two balls are on a horizontal billiard table. A 1.0 kg billiard ball moves downward along the y-axis with a speed of 16 m/s toward a 2.0 kg ball that is at rest. The balls collide at an angle, and move along the lines shown. After the collision, the 1.0 kg ball moves at 9 m/s along the $+x$-axis. The table below shows the x and y components of the momentum in kg m/s of the two balls before and after the collision.

	p_{1x}	p_{1y}	p_{2x}	p_{2y}
Before collision	0	−16	0	0
After collision	+9	0	−9	−16

159. Which of the following statements is true?

   (A) Momentum is conserved only in the x-direction in this collision.
   (B) Momentum is conserved only in the y-direction in this collision.
   (C) Momentum is conserved in both the x- and y-directions in this collision
   (D) The momentum of the 1.0 kg ball increases after the collision.
   (E) The momentum of the 2.0 kg ball decreases after the collision.

160. What is the speed of the 2.0 kg ball after the collision?

   (A) 16.0 m/s
   (B) 9.2 m/s
   (C) 7.5 m/s
   (D) 6.0 m/s
   (E) 5.0 m/s

161. A 0.3 kg baseball at rest on a tee is struck by a bat. The ball leaves the bat with a speed of 20 m/s at an angle of 45° above the horizontal. The magnitude of the impulse imparted to the baseball by the bat is most nearly

(A) 2 N s
(B) 6 N s
(C) 12 N s
(D) 16 N s
(E) 20 N s

162. Two ice skaters, a large man and a small woman, are initially at rest and holding each other's hands. They push away horizontally. Afterward, which of the following statements is true?

(A) They have equal and opposite kinetic energies.
(B) The have equal and opposite momenta.
(C) The large man applies a greater force to the small woman.
(D) The small woman applies a greater force to the large man.
(E) They recoil with equal and opposite velocities.

Questions 163–164. An object has a mass $4m$. The object explodes into three pieces of mass m, m, and $2m$. The two pieces of mass m move off at right angles to each other with the same momentum mv, as shown.

163. The speed of mass $2m$ after the explosion is

(A) $2v$

(B) $\sqrt{2}v$

(C) $\dfrac{\sqrt{2}}{2}v$

(D) $\dfrac{\sqrt{2}}{3}v$

(E) $\dfrac{\sqrt{3}}{2}v$

164. The direction of velocity of mass $2m$ is

(A) →

(B) ↙

(C) ↓

(D) ↗

(E) ↑

1 kg

2 kg

165. A system consists of two blocks having masses of 2 kg and 1 kg. The blocks are connected by a string of negligible mass and hung over a light pulley, and then released from rest. When the speed of each block is v, the momentum of the center of mass of the system is

(A) $(2 \text{ kg} + 1 \text{ kg})v$

(B) $(2 \text{ kg} - 1 \text{ kg})v$

(C) $1/3 \ (2 \text{ kg} + 1 \text{ kg})v$

(D) $\frac{1}{2} \ (2 \text{ kg} - 1 \text{ kg})v$

(E) $(2 \text{ kg})v$

Questions 166–167. A projectile is launched at an angle to the level ground as shown. At the top of the trajectory at point P, the projectile explodes into two pieces of mass $2m$ and m.

166. Which of the following arrows best represents the direction of the velocity of the center of mass of the projectile at point P after the explosion?

(A) →

(B) ↙

(C) ↘

(D) ←

(E) ↗

167. Which of the following statements is true of the center of mass of the projectile after the explosion?

(A) The center of mass will continue on a parabolic path and land on the ground at the place where it would have landed had it not exploded.

(B) The center of mass will alter its parabolic path and land on the ground farther from where it would have landed had it not exploded.

(C) The center of mass will alter its parabolic path and land on the ground at a shorter distance than it would have landed had it not exploded.

(D) The center of mass will fall straight downward from the point of explosion.

(E) The center of mass will travel straight upward from the point of explosion.

Questions 168–169. Two pieces of clay of equal mass m moving with equal speeds v_o each traveling at an angle of 30° collide and stick together at the origin O as shown.

168. Which of the following arrows represents the direction of the velocity of the combined mass after the collision?

(A) →

(B) ↓

(C) ↘

(D) ←

(E) ↑

169. The speed of the combined mass after the collision is

(A) v_o

(B) ½ v_o

(C) ¼ v_o

(D) $\dfrac{\sqrt{2}}{2} v_o$

(E) $\dfrac{\sqrt{2}}{3} v_o$

170. A small mass m is moving with a speed v toward a stationary mass $2m$. The speed of the center of mass of the system is

(A) $\left(\dfrac{m}{m+2m}\right) v$

(B) $\left(\dfrac{m+2m}{m}\right) v$

(C) $\left(\dfrac{m}{2m}\right) v$

(D) $\left(1+\dfrac{m}{2m}\right) v$

(E) $\left(1+\dfrac{2m}{m}\right) v$

Questions 171–172. Three identical masses can slide freely on a horizontal surface as shown. The first mass moves with a speed of 3.0 m/s toward the second and third masses, which are initially at rest. The first and second mass collide elastically, and then the second and third masses collide inelastically.

171. The speed of the second mass after the collision is

(A) zero
(B) 1.5 m/s
(C) 3.0 m/s
(D) 6.0 m/s
(E) 9.0 m/s

172. The speed of the second and third masses after they collide inelastically is

(A) zero
(B) 1.5 m/s
(C) 3.0 m/s
(D) 6.0 m/s
(E) 9.0 m/s

173. The diagram in the figure shows the top view of two identical steel balls on a horizontal table of negligible friction. The first ball moves with a speed of 12 m/s and the second ball is initially at rest. After the collision, the first ball moves with a speed of 8 m/s at an angle of 37° to the vertical. Which of the following diagrams best represents the approximate speed and direction of the second ball after the collision?

(A)

(B)

(C)

(D)

(E)

174. A known force **F** acts on an unknown mass for a known time Δt. From this information, you could determine the

(A) change in kinetic energy of the object
(B) change in velocity of the object
(C) acceleration of the object
(D) mass of the object
(E) change in momentum of the object

175. A block of mass m is moving to the right with a speed v_0 on a horizontal surface of negligible friction when it explodes. The explosion causes the block to break into two pieces, each of which moves in the horizontal direction. One piece of mass $m/4$ moves to the left with a speed of $2v_0$. What is the velocity of the other piece?

(A) $2v_0$ to the right
(B) v_0 to the right
(C) ¾ v_0 to the right
(D) ½ v_0 to the right
(E) ¼ v_0 to the left

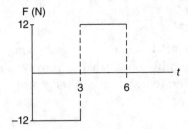

Questions 176–177. The graph shown indicates the force acting on a mass of 2 kg as a function of time.

176. For the time interval from $t = 0$ to $t = 6$ s, the change in momentum of the 2 kg mass is

(A) 48 kg m/s
(B) 24 kg m/s
(C) 12 kg m/s
(D) −12 kg m/s
(E) zero

177. If the object starts from rest, the speed at the end of the time interval from $t = 0$ to $t = 3$ s is

(A) zero
(B) 12 m/s
(C) 18 m/s
(D) 24 m/s
(E) 36 m/s

178. A 100 kg cannon sits at rest with a 1 kg cannonball in the barrel. The cannonball is fired with a speed of 50 m/s to the right, causing the cannon to recoil with a speed of 0.5 m/s to the left. The velocity of the center of mass of the cannon-cannonball system is

(A) zero
(B) 5 m/s to the right
(C) 5 m/s to the left
(D) 50 m/s to the right
(E) 50 m/s to the left

179. The vector shown represents the initial momentum of a moving object. The object collides with another object that is initially at rest. Which of the diagrams below could represent the momenta of the colliding objects after the collision?

(A)

(B)

(C)

(D)

(E)

Questions 180–181. A 20 kg boy runs at a speed of 3.0 m/s and jumps onto a 40 kg sled on frictionless ice that is initially at rest. The boy and the sled then move together for a short time.

180. The speed of the boy and sled after he jumps on it is

(A) 0.5 m/s
(B) 0.8 m/s
(C) 1.0 m/s
(D) 1.5 m/s
(E) 2.0 m/s

181. While the boy and sled are moving, he jumps off the back of the sled in such a way the boy is at rest, and the sled continues to move forward. The speed of the sled after the boy jumps off is

(A) 1.5 m/s
(B) 2.0 m/s
(C) 3.0 m/s
(D) 4.5 m/s
(E) 6.0 m/s

Questions 182–183

A cart of mass m_1 is initially moving with a speed of 4.0 m/s on a track toward a stationary cart of mass $m_2 = 2$ kg. After the collision, mass m_1 moves with a velocity of 1.5 m/s. The force vs. time graph is shown for the time during the collision, with the collision beginning at $t = 0$.

182. The impulse each cart applies to the other is most nearly

(A) 40 N s
(B) 20 N s
(C) 10 N s
(D) 5 N s
(E) 2 N s

183. The unknown mass m_1 is equal to

(A) 0.5 kg
(B) 1.5 kg
(C) 2.5 kg
(D) 4.0 kg
(E) 5.0 kg

184. A 1.0 kg block is released from rest from a height h at the top of a fixed curved ramp of negligible friction. The block slides down the ramp and collides with another block of mass 1.5 kg at rest at the bottom of the ramp. The two blocks stick together and move with a speed of 5 m/s. The height h from which the 1.0 kg block began is

(A) 0.8 m
(B) 1.2 m
(C) 1.8 m
(D) 2.8 m
(E) 7.8 m

185. A dart of mass m is fired into a wooden block of mass $4m$ that hangs from a string. The dart and block then rise to a maximum height h. An expression for the initial speed v_0 of the dart before striking the block is

(A) $\sqrt{gh}$

(B) $\sqrt{2gh}$

(C) $\sqrt{50gh}$

(D) $\sqrt{100gh}$

(E) $\sqrt{250gh}$

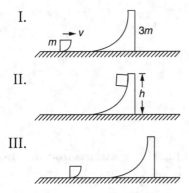

Questions 186–187. A small block of mass m slides on a horizontal frictionless surface toward a ramp of mass $3m$ which is also free to move on the surface. The small block slides up to a height h on the ramp with no friction (Figure I), then they move together (Figure II), and the small block slides back down the ramp to the horizontal surface (Figure III). Both the block and the ramp continue to slide on the horizontal surface after they separate.

186. Which of the following is true regarding the conservation laws throughout this process?

(A) Kinetic energy is conserved from Figure I to Figure II.
(B) Momentum is conserved from Figure I to Figure III.
(C) Kinetic energy is conserved from Figure II to Figure III.
(D) Potential energy is conserved from Figure I to Figure II.
(E) Potential energy is conserved from Figure II to Figure III.

187. Which of the following is a true statement regarding Figure III?

(A) The small block is moving to the left and the ramp is moving to the right.
(B) The small block is moving to the right and the ramp is moving to the left.
(C) The small block is moving to the right and the ramp is moving to the right.
(D) The small block is moving to the left and the ramp is moving to the left.
(E) The small block and the large block are moving with the same velocity.

Questions 188–189. A rubber ball of mass m is released from rest from a height h onto a fixed inclined plane angled at 45° to the horizontal. The ball collides with the surface elastically.

188. Which of the following diagrams best indicates the direction of the impulse vector **J** as it strikes the plane and the velocity vector **v** just after it strikes the plane?

    (A) →J
        →v

    (B) ↗J
        ↗v

    (C) ↗J
        ↑v

    (D) ↑J
        ↗v

    (E) ↗J
        →v

189. The speed of the ball just after striking the surface is

    (A) $\sqrt{gh}$

    (B) $\sqrt{2gh}$

    (C) $\sqrt{5gh}$

    (D) $\sqrt{7gh}$

    (E) $\sqrt{10gh}$

190. A 1000 kg (empty mass) railroad car is rolling without friction on a horizontal track at a speed of 2.0 m/s. Sand is poured into the open top of the car for the time interval from $t = 0$ to $t = 4.0$ s. The mass of the sand poured into the car as a function of time is $m(t) = 60t^2$. The velocity of the car at a time of 4.0 s is most nearly

   (A) 1 m/s
   (B) 2 m/s
   (C) 3 m/s
   (D) 4 m/s
   (E) 5 m/s

Questions 191-192. A remote controlled stunt car of mass 800 kg initially moving at 10 m/s is crashed into a rail car of mass m that is initially at rest. The cars stick together, and the speed v of both cars after the collision is given by $v = \dfrac{6}{t+1}$.

191. By considering the fact that the crash occurs at time $t = 0$, determine the mass m of the rail car.

   (A) 288 kg
   (B) 445 kg
   (C) 533 kg
   (D) 698 kg
   (E) 800 kg

192. The magnitude of the resisting force acting on the cars as a function of time after the collision is

(A) $\dfrac{6m}{t+1}$

(B) $6m(t+1)$

(C) $6m(t+1)^2$

(D) $\dfrac{6m}{(t+1)^2}$

(E) $\dfrac{m(t+1)^2}{6}$

193. A force acts on a mass m according to the equation $F = 12t^3$. If the object starts from rest, the velocity of the object as a function of time is

(A) $36mt^3$

(B) $\dfrac{36m}{t^3}$

(C) $\dfrac{mt^3}{36}$

(D) $\dfrac{t^3}{3m}$

(E) $\dfrac{3t^4}{m}$

194. A dart in a long blow gun starts from rest and gains a momentum according to the equation $p = 3t^3 + 2t$ while moving through the barrel of the gun. The net force acting on the dart after 0.2 s is

(A) 1.2 N

(B) 2.4 N

(C) 6.0 N

(D) 12.2 N

(E) 16.1 N

195. A variable force acts on a mass causing it to accelerate. If a graph of this force vs. time is plotted, the change in momentum of the mass can be determined by finding the
    (A) slope of the graph
    (B) area under the graph
    (C) y-intercept of the graph
    (D) x-intercept of the graph
    (E) change in slope of the graph

196. A moving object is changing its momentum during a time interval. If a graph of momentum vs. time is plotted, the net force acting on the mass at any time can be determined by finding the
    (A) slope of line tangent to the graph at that time
    (B) area under the graph
    (C) y-intercept of the graph
    (D) x-intercept of the graph
    (E) change in slope of the graph from beginning to end

Free Response

Questions 197–200. Two blocks rest on a smooth table that is 1.5 m high. Block A has a mass $m_A = 2$ kg and block B has a mass $m_B = 4$ kg. Block A is then given a velocity of 4 m/s toward block B, and they collide and stick together.

197. Determine the speed of the two blocks immediately after they collide inelastically.

198. Determine the horizontal distance the two blocks travel before striking the floor.

Similar to the previous questions, two blocks rest on a smooth table that is 1.5 m high. Block A has a mass $m_A = 2$ kg and block B has a mass $m_B = 4$ kg. Block A is then given a velocity of 4.0 m/s toward block B, and they collide *elastically*. Block A rebounds with a velocity of -1.0 m/s.

199. Determine the speed of block B immediately after they collide elastically.

200. Determine the horizontal distance block B travels before striking the floor.

CHAPTER 5

Circular and Rotational Motion

On all of the questions in this book, you may neglect air resistance and use $g = 10$ m/s^2 unless otherwise noted.

201. Linear acceleration is to force as angular acceleration is to

(A) kinetic energy
(B) angular velocity
(C) rotational inertia
(D) torque
(E) angular momentum

202. A girl stands on a rotating merry-go-round without holding on to a rail. The force that keeps her moving in a circle is the

(A) frictional force on the girl directed away from the center of the merry-go-round
(B) frictional force on the girl directed toward the center of the merry-go-round
(C) normal force on the girl directed away from the center of the merry-go-round
(D) normal force on the girl directed toward the center of the merry-go-round
(E) weight of the girl

203. A 0.5 kg ball on the end of a 0.5 m long string is swung in a horizontal circle. What would the speed of the ball have to be for the tension in the string to be 9.0 N?

(A) 1.0 m/s
(B) 3.0 m/s
(C) 6.0 m/s
(D) 9.0 m/s
(E) 12.0 m/s

Questions 204–205. A ball of mass *m* and weight *W* on the end of a string is swung in a horizontal circle of radius *R* with a speed *v*. The string makes an angle θ below the horizontal, as shown. The magnitude of the tension in the string is *T*.

204. Which of the following diagrams best shows the forces acting on the ball as it moves in a circle?

(A)

(B)

(C)

(D)

(E)

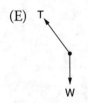

205. In terms of m, R, v, and θ, the magnitude of the tension T is

(A) $\dfrac{mv^2}{R}$

(B) $\dfrac{mv^2}{R\sin\theta}$

(C) $\dfrac{mv^2}{R\cos\theta}$

(D) $\dfrac{mv}{R\sin\theta}$

(E) $mvR\sin\theta$

206. A ball of mass m is swung in a vertical circle of radius R. The speed of the ball at the bottom of the circle is v. The tension in the string at the bottom of the circle is

(A) mg

(B) $mg + \dfrac{mv^2}{R}$

(C) $mg - \dfrac{mv^2}{R}$

(D) $\dfrac{mv^2}{R}$

(E) zero

207. A car of mass m drives on a flat circular track of radius R. To maintain a constant speed v on the track, the coefficient of friction μ between the tires and the road must be

(A) mg

(B) $mg + \dfrac{mv^2}{R}$

(C) $mg - \dfrac{mv^2}{R}$

(D) $\dfrac{v^2}{gR}$

(E) $\sqrt{\dfrac{v^2}{gR}}$

Front view

Questions 208–209. A race car travels on a circular track that is banked at an angle θ from the horizontal, as shown.

208. Which of the following diagrams best shows the forces acting on the car as it moves on the banked track?

(A)

(B)

(C)

(D)

(E)

209. Which of the following statements is true of the forces acting on the car while on the circular track?

(A) The normal force the track exerts on the car provides the centripetal force.

(B) The weight of the car provides the centripetal force.

(C) The frictional force the track exerts on the car provides the centripetal force.

(D) The centripetal force is provided by a combination of the normal force and frictional force.

(E) There is no centripetal force in this case.

210. A meter stick of mass 0.1 kg rests on a table as shown. A length of 40 cm extends over the edge of the table. How far from the edge of the table could a 0.05 kg mass be placed on the meter stick so that the stick just begins to tip?

(A) 5 cm

(B) 10 cm

(C) 15 cm

(D) 20 cm

(E) 30 cm

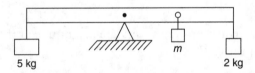

211. A meter stick is balanced on a fulcrum at its center, as shown. A mass of 5 kg is hung on the left end of the stick, and a mass of 2 kg is hung on the right end. In order to balance the system, a mass m is hung at the 25-cm mark on the right side. What is the value of the mass m?

(A) 12 kg

(B) 6 kg

(C) 4 kg

(D) 3 kg

(E) 2 kg

Questions 212–213. A 3 kg object moves in a horizontal circle of radius 3 m with a constant speed of 2 m/s.

212. The net force acting on the object is

    (A) 18 N

    (B) 12 N

    (C) 9 N

    (D) 6 N

    (E) 4 N

213. The angular momentum of the object is

    (A) 18 kg m^2/s

    (B) 12 kg m^2/s

    (C) 9 kg m^2/s

    (D) 6 kg m^2/s

    (E) 4 kg m^2/s

Questions 214–215. The diagram above shows a force **F** being applied at an angle θ to a rod that is pivoted at one end and is free to rotate without friction in a horizontal plane.

214. Which of the following equations represents the magnitude of the net torque τ acting on the rod?

    (A) FR

    (B) $FR\cos\theta$

    (C) $FR\sin\theta$

    (D) $FR\tan\theta$

    (E) $\dfrac{FR}{\cos\theta}$

215. If the angle θ remains constant as the rod turns on its axis, and the rotational inertia of the rod is I, the angular acceleration of the rod is

(A) $\dfrac{FR}{I}$

(B) $\dfrac{I}{FR\cos\theta}$

(C) $\dfrac{FR\sin\theta}{I}$

(D) $\dfrac{FR\tan\theta}{I}$

(E) $\dfrac{FR\cos\theta}{I}$

216. A ballet dancer is spinning around a vertical axis with her arms fully extended. How are her angular momentum and kinetic energy affected as she pulls her arms in toward her body as she spins?

(A) Her angular momentum remains constant, but her kinetic energy increases.

(B) Her angular momentum increases, but her kinetic energy remains constant.

(C) Her angular momentum decreases, but her kinetic energy remains constant.

(D) Her angular momentum increases, but her kinetic energy decreases.

(E) Both her angular momentum and kinetic energy remain constant.

Questions 217–218. A ball on the end of a string is swung in a circle of radius 2 m according to the equation $\theta = 4t^2 + 3t$, where θ is in radians and t is in seconds.

217. The angular acceleration of the ball is

(A) 6 rad/s^2

(B) $4t^2 + 3t$ rad/s^2

(C) $8t + 3$ rad/s^2

(D) $\frac{3}{4} t^3 + 3 t^2$ rad/s^2

(E) 8 rad/s^2

218. The linear speed v of the ball at $t = 3$ s is

(A) 27 m/s

(B) 54 m/s

(C) 108 m/s

(D) 135 m/s

(E) 210 m/s

219. A metal bar of constant density and weight W is attached to a pivot on the wall at point P and supported by a rope that makes an angle of 60° with the vertical wall. The reaction force exerted by the pivot on the bar at point P is best represented by which arrow?

(A) ↗

(B) ↑

(C) ↓

(D) ↖

(E) ↘

220. A particle of mass m moves with a constant speed v at a distance x_o parallel to the y-axis as shown. When the particle is in the position shown, the magnitude of its angular momentum relative to the origin is

(A) mvx_o

(B) mvy_o

(C) $mv\sqrt{x_o^2 + y_o^2}$

(D) $\dfrac{mv}{\sqrt{x_o^2 + y_o^2}}$

(E) zero

221. A uniform rod of length L and mass m has a rotational inertia of $1/12\ mL^2$ about its center. A particle, also of mass m, is attached to one end of the stick. The combined rotational inertia of the stick and particle about the center of the rod is

(A) $\dfrac{mL^2}{3}$

(B) $\dfrac{12mL^2}{13}$

(C) $\dfrac{13mL^2}{12}$

(D) $\dfrac{mL^2}{156}$

(E) $\dfrac{13mL^2}{156}$

Questions 222–223. A light rod of negligible mass is pivoted at point P a distance L from one end as shown. A mass m is attached to the left end of the rod at a distance of $3L$ from the pivot, and another mass $4m$ is attached to the other end a distance L from the pivot. The system begins from rest in the horizontal position.

222. The net torque acting on the system due to gravitational forces is

(A) $4mgL$ clockwise

(B) $3mgL$ clockwise

(C) $3mgL$ counterclockwise

(D) mgL counterclockwise

(E) mgL clockwise

223. The angular acceleration of the system when it is released from rest is

(A) zero

(B) $\dfrac{g}{5L}$

(C) $\dfrac{g}{4L}$

(D) $\dfrac{g}{13L}$

(E) $\dfrac{g}{L}$

224. A hoop of radius R and mass m has a rotational inertia of mR^2. The hoop rolls without slipping along a horizontal floor with a constant speed v and then rolls up a long incline. The hoop can roll up the incline to a maximum vertical height of

(A) $\dfrac{v^2}{g}$

(B) $\dfrac{2v^2}{g}$

(C) $\dfrac{v^2}{2g}$

(D) $\dfrac{4v^2}{g}$

(E) $\dfrac{v^2}{4g}$

225. A ball on the end of a string is released from rest at point X as shown. The ball swings under the influence of gravity from point X through points Y and Z. What are the directions of the acceleration vectors at points Y and Z, respectively?

(A) Point Y: ↑   Point Z: ←

(B) Point Y: ↓   Point Z: ↓

(C) Point Y: ↖   Point Z: ↘

(D) Point Y: ↘   Point Z: ←

(E) Point Y: ↑   Point Z: ↘

226. A force **F** is applied at the end of a rod of length L, creating a counterclockwise torque as shown. Which of the following diagrams shows a force that can create the same torque about point O?

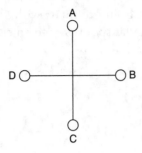

Questions 227–228. Two balls of equal mass are attached to each end of a rod that is spinning about its center in the vertical plane with a constant angular speed ω. Each ball is a radius r from the center of the rod. A bug holds on to one of the balls as the system rotates. Four points, A, B, C, and D, are marked at the quarter circle points on the circle.

227. At which point would the bug need to apply the most adhesive force to remain on the ball?

(A) A
(B) B
(C) C
(D) D
(E) The bug would apply the same force at all points to remain on the ball.

228. The minimum force necessary the bug would have to apply to remain on the ball at point C is

(A) $m\omega r$
(B) $m\omega^2 r$
(C) mg
(D) $m\omega^2 r - mg$
(E) $m\omega^2 r + mg$

229. A merry-go-round is initially at rest, and begins to rotate with a constant angular acceleration α. The angular speed ω of the merry-go-round after making two complete revolutions is

(A) 2α
(B) 4α
(C) $\sqrt{2\pi\alpha}$
(D) $4\pi\alpha$
(E) $\sqrt{8\pi\alpha}$

230. Two disks are fixed to a vertical axle that is rotating with a constant angular speed ω. The smaller disk has a mass m and a radius r, and the larger disk has a mass $2m$ and radius $2r$. The general equation for the rotational inertia of a disk of mass M and radius R is $\frac{1}{2} MR^2$. The ratio of the angular momentum of the larger disk to the smaller disk is

(A) 1/4
(B) 4/1
(C) 1/2
(D) 2/1
(E) 8/1

3 kg   6 kg

A   B   C   D   E

231. A light rod has a mass attached at each end. At one end is a 6 kg mass, and at the other end is a 3 kg mass. An axis can be placed at any of the points shown. Through which point should an axis be placed so that the rotational inertia is the greatest about that axis?

(A) A
(B) B
(C) C
(D) D
(E) E

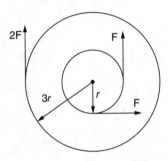

232. Two wheels are attached to each other and fixed so that they can only turn together. The smaller wheel has a radius of r and the larger wheel has a radius of $3r$. The two wheels can rotate together on a frictionless axle. Three forces act tangentially on the edge of the wheels as shown. The magnitude of the net torque acting on the system of wheels is

(A) Fr
(B) $2Fr$
(C) $3Fr$
(D) $4Fr$
(E) $6Fr$

233. A speed skater races around a track in which the sides are equal length and parallel and the curves are semicircular. The skater keeps a constant speed throughout one entire lap. She starts at point A and travels counterclockwise around the track for one lap. Which of the following graphs best represents the magnitude of the skater's acceleration as a function of time for one lap?

(A)

(B)

(C)

(D)

(E)

Questions 234–235. A disk is mounted on a fixed axle. The rotational inertia of the disk is I. The angular velocity of the disk is decreased from ω_o to ω_f during a time Δt due to friction in the axle.

234. The magnitude of the average net torque acting on the wheel is

(A) $\dfrac{(\omega_f - \omega_o)}{\Delta t}$

(B) $\dfrac{(\omega_f - \omega_o)^2}{\Delta t}$

(C) $\dfrac{I(\omega_f - \omega_o)}{\Delta t}$

(D) $\dfrac{I(\omega_f - \omega_o)^2}{\Delta t}$

(E) $\dfrac{I(\omega_f - \omega_o)}{\Delta t^2}$

235. The average power developed by the friction in the axle of the disk to bring it to a complete stop is

(A) $\dfrac{\omega_o}{\Delta t}$

(B) $\dfrac{(\omega_o)^2}{\Delta t}$

(C) $\dfrac{I(\omega_f - \omega_o)}{\Delta t}$

(D) $\dfrac{I(\omega_o)^2}{\Delta t}$

(E) $\dfrac{I(\omega_f - \omega_o)}{\Delta t^2}$

236. A string is pulled through a hole in a horizontal table. A puck of mass m is attached to one end of the string so that it can move in a circle of radius r on the smooth tabletop with a speed v, and a weight hangs from the other end under the table. If the weight is pulled down so that the length of the string is shortened to ¼ r while the puck is moving in a circle, the speed of the puck will

(A) decrease its speed to ¼ v
(B) decrease its speed to ½ v
(C) increase its speed to $2v$
(D) increase its speed to $4v$
(E) not change

237. A billiard ball of mass m and radius r rolls without slipping on a pool table with an angular speed ω. Which of the following relationships is true of the ball as it rolls?

(A) $v = r\omega$
(B) $v > r\omega$
(C) $v < r\omega$
(D) $v = 2r\omega$
(E) $v = ½\, r\omega$

238. A billiard ball of mass m and radius r rolls and slips on a pool table with an angular speed ω. Which of the following relationships is true of the ball as it rolls and slips?

(A) $v = r\omega$
(B) $v > r\omega$
(C) $v < r\omega$
(D) $v = 2r\omega$
(E) $v = ½\, r\omega$

239. An amusement park ride consists of a cylindrical room that spins so that people leaning up against the wall can stick to the wall even if the floor is lowered out from under them. The rotating room reaches a maximum angular speed ω, the floor is lowered, and the riders stick to the wall. Which of the following statements is true?

(A) The weight of each rider provides the centripetal force keeping the rider moving in a circle.

(B) The normal force applied by the wall must equal the weight of the rider.

(C) The difference between the normal force applied by the wall and the weight of the rider is equal to the centripetal force acting on the rider.

(D) The frictional force between the wall and the rider must equal the weight of the rider.

(E) The frictional force between the wall and the rider provides the centripetal force acting on the rider.

240. Astronauts are conducting an experiment in a negligible gravity environment. Two spheres of mass m are attached to either end of a light rod. As the rod and spheres float motionless in space, an astronaut launches a piece of sticky clay, also of mass m, toward one of the spheres so that the clay strikes and sticks to the sphere perpendicular to the rod. Which of the following statements is true of the motion of the rod, clay, and spheres after the collision?

(A) Linear momentum is not conserved, but angular momentum is conserved.

(B) Angular momentum is not conserved, but linear momentum is conserved.

(C) Kinetic energy is conserved, but angular momentum is not conserved.

(D) Kinetic energy is conserved, but linear momentum is not conserved.

(E) Both linear momentum and angular momentum are conserved, but kinetic energy is not conserved.

241. A rod of mass M, length L, and rotational inertia I hangs at rest from a frictionless axle as shown. A ball of mass m with a speed v strikes the rod perpendicularly at the end of the rod. As a result of the collision, the ball stops. The angular speed of the rod immediately after the collision is

(A) vL

(B) $\dfrac{v}{L}$

(C) $\dfrac{mv}{I}$

(D) $\dfrac{mvL}{I}$

(E) $\dfrac{mv}{IL}$

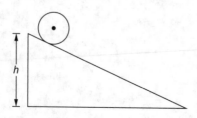

Questions 242–243

A hollow sphere of mass m and radius R begins from rest at a height h and rolls down a rough inclined plane. The rotational inertia of the hollow sphere is $2/3\ mR^2$.

242. Which of the following diagrams best represents the forces acting on the sphere as it rolls down the plane?

(A)

(B)

(C)

(D)

(E)

243. The speed of the sphere when it reaches the bottom of the plane is

(A) $\sqrt{\dfrac{8gh}{5}}$

(B) $\sqrt{\dfrac{6gh}{5}}$

(C) $\sqrt{\dfrac{5gh}{6}}$

(D) $\sqrt{\dfrac{7gh}{10}}$

(E) $\sqrt{\dfrac{gh}{2}}$

244. A belt is wrapped around two wheels as shown. The smaller wheel has a radius r, and the larger wheel has a radius $2r$. When the wheels turn, the belt does not slip on the wheels, and gives the smaller wheel an angular speed ω. The angular speed of the larger wheel is

(A) ω

(B) 2ω

(C) $\frac{1}{2}\,\omega$

(D) $\frac{1}{4}\,\omega$

(E) 4ω

245. One end of a stick of length L, rotational inertia I, and mass m is pivoted on an axle with negligible friction at point P. The other end is tied to a string and held in a horizontal position. When the string is cut, the stick rotates counterclockwise. The angular speed ω of the stick when it reaches the bottom of its swing is

(A) $\dfrac{mgL}{I}$

(B) $\sqrt{\dfrac{mgL}{I}}$

(C) $\sqrt{\dfrac{2mgL}{I}}$

(D) $\sqrt{\dfrac{mgL}{2I}}$

(E) $\sqrt{\dfrac{4mgL}{I}}$

Free Response

Questions 246–247

A mass m is hung on a string that is wrapped around a disk of radius R and rotational inertia I. The mass is released from rest and accelerates downward with an acceleration a.

246. Determine the tension in the string as the mass accelerates downward in terms of the given quantities.

247. In terms of the tension T and the other given quantities, determine the rate of change of the angular speed of the disk.

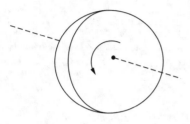

Questions 248–250. A disk having a rotational inertia of 2 kg m^2 rotates about a fixed axis through its center. The disk begins from rest at $t = 0$, and at time $t = 2$ s, its angular velocity is 2 rad/s.

248. Determine the angular momentum of the disk at $t = 2$ s.

249. What is the angular acceleration of the disk between $t = 0$ and $t = 2$ s?

250. What is the kinetic energy of the disk at $t = 2$ s?

CHAPTER 6

Oscillations and Gravitation

On all of the questions in this book, you may neglect air resistance and use $g = 10 \text{ m/s}^2$ unless otherwise noted.

251. A simple pendulum has a mass m, length L, and period T. If the pendulum mass is replaced by a mass of $2m$, the period will be

(A) doubled
(B) halved
(C) quartered
(D) quadrupled
(E) unchanged

252. A mass oscillates on the end of a spring that obeys Hooke's law. Which of the following statements is true?

(A) The amplitude of oscillation is equal to the potential energy of the spring.
(B) The kinetic energy of the oscillating mass is constant.
(C) The maximum potential energy occurs when the mass reaches the equilibrium position.
(D) The potential energy of the spring at the amplitude is equal to the kinetic energy at the equilibrium position.
(E) The kinetic energy of the spring at the amplitude is equal to the potential energy at the equilibrium position.

Questions 253–254

A mass of 1 kg is hung on a spring that is held at its unstretched length. The constant of the spring is 20 N/m. The mass is released from rest.

253. The mass falls to an amplitude of

(A) ½ m

(B) 1/20 m

(C) ¼ m

(D) 1/40 m

(E) 1.0 m

254. The period of the oscillation is

(A) $2\pi\sqrt{\dfrac{1}{40}}$ s

(B) $2\pi\sqrt{\dfrac{1}{20}}$ s

(C) $2\pi\sqrt{\dfrac{1}{400}}$ s

(D) $2\pi\sqrt{\dfrac{1}{200}}$ s

(E) $2\pi\sqrt{\dfrac{1}{10}}$ s

255. A superball is dropped from a height of 5.0 meters above a floor. The ball bounces off the floor in a perfectly elastic collision so that it rises to the same height with each bounce. The motion of the ball can be described as

(A) harmonic motion with a period of 2 s
(B) harmonic motion with a period of 1 s
(C) harmonic motion with a period of ½ s
(D) motion with a constant velocity
(E) motion with a constant momentum

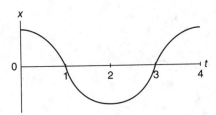

Questions 256–257
A position vs. time graph is shown above for an object in simple harmonic motion.

256. Which of the following kinetic energy vs. time graphs best represents the motion of the object?

(A)

(B)

(C)

(D)

(E)

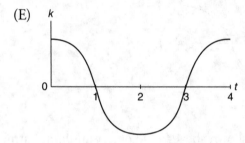

257. Which of the following potential energy vs. time graphs best represents the motion of the object?

(A)

(B)

(C)

(D)

(E)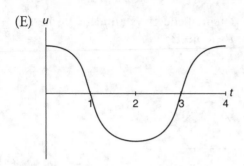

258. An object oscillates in simple harmonic motion along the x-axis according to the equation $x = 6\cos(4t)$. The period of oscillation of the object is

(A) ¼ s
(B) 4 s
(C) $\pi/4$ s
(D) $\pi/2$ s
(E) 4π s

259. A mass m oscillates on the end of a string of length L. The frequency of the pendulum is f. How would you increase the frequency of the pendulum to $2f$?

(A) Increase the length of the pendulum to $4L$
(B) Decrease the length of the pendulum to $\frac{1}{4}L$
(C) Increase the length of the pendulum to $2L$
(D) Decrease the length of the pendulum to $\frac{1}{2}L$
(E) Decrease the mass of the pendulum to $\frac{1}{2} m$

260. A mass hangs from two parallel springs, each with the same spring
constant k. Compared to the period T of the same mass oscillating
on one of the springs, the period of oscillation of the mass with both
springs connected to it is

(A) ¼ T
(B) ½ T
(C) T (unchanged)
(D) $2T$
(E) $4T$

261. Which of the following is generally true for an object in simple
harmonic motion on a spring of constant k?

(A) The greater the spring constant k, the greater the amplitude of
the motion.
(B) The greater the spring constant k, the greater the period of the
motion.
(C) The greater the spring constant k, the greater the frequency of
the motion.
(D) The lower the spring constant k, the greater the frequency of
the motion.
(E) The lower the spring constant k, the greater the kinetic energy
of the motion.

Questions 262–263

A mass m oscillates in simple harmonic motion along the x-axis on a spring of constant k.

262. Which of the following best represents the differential equation that describes the motion of the mass as it oscillates?

(A) $\dfrac{d^2x}{dt^2} = -\dfrac{k}{m}x$

(B) $\dfrac{dx}{dt} = -\dfrac{k}{m}x$

(C) $\dfrac{dx}{dt} = -\dfrac{m}{k}x$

(D) $\dfrac{d^2x}{dt^2} = -\dfrac{m}{k}x$

(E) $\dfrac{d^2x}{dt^2} = -\dfrac{dx}{dt}$

263. The position as a function of time can be expressed by the equation

(A) $x = x_o \cos kt$

(B) $x = x_o \cos \pi t$

(C) $x = x_o \cos \sqrt{\dfrac{k}{m}}\, t$

(D) $x = x_o \cos \sqrt{\dfrac{m}{k}}\, t$

(E) $x = x_o \cos \dfrac{k}{m}\, t$

Questions 264–266

A harmonic oscillator follows the equation $\dfrac{d^2x}{dt^2} = -4x$. The spring constant k is 4 N/m.

264. The angular frequency ω of the harmonic motion is

(A) zero

(B) 2 rad/s

(C) 4 rad/s

(D) 8 rad/s

(E) 16 rad/s

265. The mass m oscillating on the spring is

(A) 1 kg
(B) 2 kg
(C) 4 kg
(D) 8 kg
(E) 16 kg

266. The period T of oscillation is

(A) zero
(B) $\pi/4$ s
(C) $\pi/2$ s
(D) π s
(E) 2π s

267. A pendulum of length L has a period of 2 s on Earth. A planetary explorer takes the same pendulum of length L to another planet where its period is 1 s. The gravitational acceleration on the surface of this planet is most nearly

(A) $8\,g$
(B) $4\,g$
(C) $2\,g$
(D) $\frac{1}{2}\,g$
(E) $\frac{1}{4}\,g$

268. A block of mass m is attached to a spring fixed to a wall. The mass oscillates on a frictionless horizontal surface with an amplitude x_0. The force constant of the spring is k. In terms of the given quantities, what is the maximum speed of the block?

(A) $\dfrac{k}{m}x_0$

(B) $\sqrt{\dfrac{k}{m}x_0}$

(C) $\sqrt{\dfrac{k}{m}}\,x_0$

(D) kmx_0

(E) $\dfrac{x_0}{m}k$

269. A block of mass 1.0 kg is sliding on a frictionless horizontal surface with a speed of 4.0 m/s when it collides inelastically with another 1.0 kg block attached to a spring. The spring compresses a distance of 0.5 m after the collision. The force constant k of the spring is

(A) 2 N/m
(B) 4 N/m
(C) 8 N/m
(D) 16 N/m
(E) 32 N/m

270. A block of mass 0.5 kg rests up against a compressed spring of force constant 5 N/m. The spring is released, and the block travels a distance of 1.0 m when the block leaves the spring at the edge of the horizontal frictionless table, and is projected to the floor. The table is 1.5 m high. The horizontal distance from the table the block lands on the floor is

(A) 1.2 m
(B) 1.7 m
(C) 2.1 m
(D) 2.8 m
(E) 3.4 m

271. A mass moving with a velocity v travels toward another mass on a frictionless air track. The mass at rest has an ideal spring attached to it. The moving mass collides elastically with the mass at rest, compressing the spring, then bouncing back. Which of the following graphs best represents the kinetic energy vs. time graph before, during, and after the collision?

(A)

(B)

(C)

(D)

(E)

272. A satellite orbits the Earth at a distance that is four times the radius of the Earth. If the acceleration due to gravity near the surface of the Earth is g, the acceleration of the satellite is most nearly

(A) zero
(B) $g/2$
(C) $g/4$
(D) $g/8$
(E) $g/16$

273. The mass of a planet is ¼ that of Earth and its radius is half of Earth's radius. The acceleration due to gravity on this planet is most nearly

(A) 2 m/s²
(B) 4 m/s²
(C) 5 m/s²
(D) 10 m/s²
(E) 20 m/s²

B • A

274. A satellite orbits the Earth in an elliptical orbit, with point A being close to the Earth and point B farther away. As the satellite moves from point A to point B, which of the following is true of the angular momentum and kinetic energy of the satellite?

	Angular Momentum	Kinetic Energy
(A)	Increases	Remains constant
(B)	Remains constant	Increases
(C)	Decreases	Remains constant
(D)	Remains constant	Decreases
(E)	Remains constant	Remains constant

275. Two planets of mass M and $9M$ are in the same solar system. The radius of the planet of mass M is R. In order for the acceleration due to gravity to be the same for each planet, the radius of the planet of mass $9M$ would have to be

(A) ½ R
(B) R
(C) $2R$
(D) $3R$
(E) $9R$

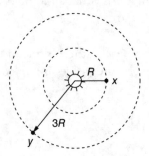

276. Two planets, X and Y, orbit a star. Planet X orbits at a radius R, and Planet Y orbits at a radius $3R$. Which of the following best represents the relationship between the acceleration a_x of Planet X and the acceleration a_Y of Planet Y?

(A) $a_x = 9a_Y$
(B) $9a_x = a_Y$
(C) $a_x = 3a_Y$
(D) $3a_x = a_Y$
(E) $a_x = a_Y$

277. A satellite is in a stable circular orbit around the Earth at a radius R and speed v. At what radius would the satellite travel in a stable orbit with a speed $2v$?

(A) ¼ R
(B) ½ R
(C) R
(D) $2R$
(E) $4R$

278. The Earth and the moon apply a gravitational force to each other. Which of the following statements is true?

(A) The Earth applies a greater force on the moon than the moon exerts on the Earth.

(B) The Earth applies a smaller force on the moon than the moon exerts on the Earth.

(C) The Earth applies a force on the moon, but the moon does not exert a force on the Earth.

(D) The Earth does not apply a force on the moon, but the moon exerts a force on the Earth.

(E) The force the Earth applies to the moon is equal and opposite to the force the moon applies to the Earth.

279. Two masses exert a gravitational force F on each other. If one of the masses is doubled, and the distance between the masses is tripled, the new force between them is

(A) $6F$

(B) $2/3\ F$

(C) $2/9\ F$

(D) $3/2\ F$

(E) $4/9\ F$

280. A planet orbits at a radius R around a star of mass M. The period of orbit of the planet is

(A) $\sqrt{\dfrac{4\pi^2 R^2}{GM}}$

(B) $\dfrac{4\pi^2 R^3}{GM}$

(C) $\sqrt{\dfrac{4\pi^2 R^3}{GM}}$

(D) $\sqrt{\dfrac{4\pi^2 R}{GM}}$

(E) $\dfrac{GM}{4\pi^2 R}$

281. A moon orbits a large planet in an elliptical orbit, with its closest approach at a distance *a*, and its farthest distance *b*. The speed of the moon at point *b* is *v*. The speed at point *a* is

(A) $\dfrac{av}{b}$

(B) $\dfrac{bv}{a}$

(C) $\dfrac{(a+b)v}{b}$

(D) $\dfrac{(b-a)v}{b}$

(E) $\dfrac{2bv}{a}$

Questions 282–283

Two masses are initially a very large distance apart. The masses are allowed to accelerate toward one another due to the gravitational force between them.

282. Which of the following best represents the potential energy *U* as a function of distance *r* as the masses move toward each other?

(A)

(B)

(C)

(D)

(E)

283. Which of the following best represents the potential energy U as a function of time t as the masses move toward each other?

(A)

(B)

(C)

(D)

(E)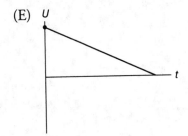

284. A satellite orbits the Earth in an elliptical orbit. Which of the following statements is true?

(A) The angular velocity of the satellite increases as it travels farther from the Earth.

(B) The acceleration of the satellite increases as it travels closer to the Earth.

(C) The angular momentum of the satellite increases as it travels closer to the Earth.

(D) The potential energy of the satellite is equal to its kinetic energy at all points in the orbit.

(E) The speed of the satellite must remain constant for it to remain in orbit around the Earth.

Questions 285–286

A satellite orbits a planet with a speed v in a circular orbit of radius R.

285. If the speed of the satellite is slightly increased, which of the
following best represents the new orbit of the satellite?

(A)

(B)

(C)

(D)

(E)

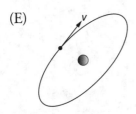

286. If the speed of the satellite is slightly decreased, which of the following best represents the new orbit of the satellite?

(A)

(B)

(C)

(D)

(E)

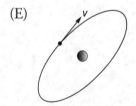

287. Two stars of equal mass M orbit around their center of mass, each with a speed v. The distance between the stars is R. Which of the following is an expression for the speed v of the stars?

(A) $\dfrac{GM}{R}$

(B) $\dfrac{GM}{R^2}$

(C) $\sqrt{\dfrac{GM}{R}}$

(D) $\sqrt{\dfrac{GM}{R^2}}$

(E) $\sqrt{\dfrac{GM}{2R}}$

288. A satellite of mass m travels in an elliptical orbit around a planet of mass M. The satellite has a speed v when it is closest to the planet at a distance r. Work is done by the engines of the satellite to change its orbit to a circular orbit when it is at this distance r. Which of the following statements is true of the transition from an elliptical orbit to a circular orbit?

(A) The work done by the satellite engines to change the orbit is equal to the change in kinetic energy of the satellite.

(B) The work done by the satellite engines to change the orbit is equal to the change in potential energy of the satellite.

(C) The work done by the satellite engines to change the orbit is equal to the change in angular momentum of the satellite.

(D) The work done by the satellite engines to change the orbit is equal to the change in speed of the satellite.

(E) The work done by the satellite engines to change the orbit is equal to the change in orbital radius of the satellite.

289. A satellite of mass m orbits the Earth with a potential energy U and a kinetic energy K. Which of the following statements would have to be true for the satellite to escape the Earth's gravity completely?

(A) The kinetic energy of the satellite would have to be equal to the potential energy between the Earth and the satellite.

(B) The potential energy between the Earth and the satellite would have to be greater than the kinetic energy of the satellite.

(C) The total energy of the satellite would have to be greater than the kinetic energy of the satellite.

(D) The kinetic energy of the satellite would have to be greater than the potential energy of the satellite.

(E) The total energy of the satellite would have to be equal to the potential energy of the satellite.

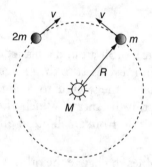

Questions 290–291

Two moons of mass m and $2m$ orbit a planet of mass M at the same radius R and speed v toward each other, as shown. The moons collide and stick together without destroying either moon.

290. The total momentum of the moons after the collision is

(A) mv

(B) $2mv$

(C) $3mv$

(D) $6mv$

(E) zero

291. The velocity of the two masses after the collision is

(A) v counterclockwise
(B) $v/2$ counterclockwise
(C) $v/2$ clockwise
(D) $v/3$ counterclockwise
(E) $v/3$ clockwise

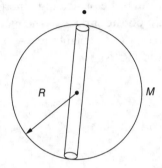

Questions 292–293

A tunnel is drilled through the diameter of a nonrotating planet of mass M and constant density, as shown. The radius of the planet is R. A small ball of mass m is dropped from rest into the hole at the surface of the planet.

292. The speed of the ball at the center of the planet is

(A) $\dfrac{GM}{R}$

(B) $\dfrac{GM}{R^2}$

(C) $\sqrt{\dfrac{2GM}{R}}$

(D) $\sqrt{\dfrac{2GM}{R^2}}$

(E) $\sqrt{\dfrac{GM}{2R}}$

293. Which of the following best describes the subsequent motion of the ball as it falls through the planet?

(A) The ball will come to rest at the center of the planet.

(B) The ball will travel through the planet and continue with a constant velocity after it leaves the planet.

(C) The ball will reverse the direction of its velocity at the center of the planet and return to the surface.

(D) The ball will travel completely through the planet and emerge on the other side, and then remain on the surface of the planet.

(E) The ball will oscillate about the center of the planet in harmonic motion with an amplitude R.

Free Response

O   A

Questions 294–295

A mass m oscillates on an ideal spring of spring constant k on a frictionless horizontal surface. The mass is pulled aside to a distance A from its equilibrium position, and released.

294. In terms of the given quantities, at what distance from the equilibrium position is the potential energy of the mass equal to its kinetic energy?

295. In terms of the given quantities, what is the acceleration of the mass when it is at the amplitude A?

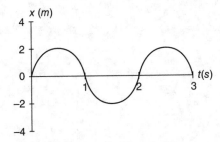

Questions 296–297

A mass oscillates in simple harmonic motion as shown by the position x vs. time t graph above.

296. What is the frequency of oscillation?

297. Write the equation that represents the speed of the mass as a function of time.

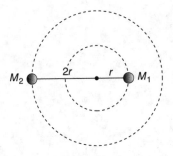

Questions 298–300

Two stars of unequal mass orbit each other about their common center of mass as shown. The star of mass M_1 orbits in a circle of radius r, and the star of mass M_2 orbits in a circle of radius $2r$.

298. Determine the ratio of masses M_1/M_2.

299. Determine the ratio of the acceleration a_1 of M_1 to the acceleration a_2 of M_2.

300. Determine the ratio of the period T_1 of M_1 to the period T_2 of M_2.

CHAPTER 7

Electric Force, Field, Potential, Gauss's Law

301. A positive charge is placed on a spherical conducting hollow shell of radius R. Which of the following statements is true?

(A) The charge is distributed evenly on the inside surface of the sphere.

(B) The charge is distributed evenly on the outside surface of the sphere.

(C) The charge is concentrated at the center of the sphere.

(D) The inside surface of the sphere is negatively charged.

(E) The charge is concentrated at the poles on the surface of the sphere.

302. A negative charge is placed on a solid conducting sphere of radius R. Which of the following statements is true?

(A) The electric field is zero everywhere inside the sphere.

(B) The electric field is zero just outside the surface of the sphere.

(C) The electric field is maximum at the center of the sphere.

(D) The electric field is directed radially outward outside the surface of the sphere.

(E) The electric field inside the sphere is equal and opposite to the electric field outside the surface of the sphere.

Questions 303–304

The shape shown is made of a solid conducting material of constant density. A positive charge is placed on the surface of the shape.

303. Which of the following diagrams best represents the distribution of charge on the surface of the shape?

(A)

(B)

(C)

(D)

(E)

304. Which of the following statements is true?

(A) The electric field must be uniform everywhere on the surface of the shape.

(B) The electric field must be equal inside and outside the shape.

(C) The electric potential must be uniform everywhere on the surface of the shape.

(D) The charge must be equal both inside and outside the shape, but opposite in sign.

(E) The charge must be equal both inside and outside the shape, having the same sign.

−3 μC   +1 μC

305. Two conducting spheres of equal radius are separated by a distance *r* as shown. A charge of −3 *μC* is placed on one of the spheres and a charge of +1 *μC* is placed on the other sphere so that the force between them has a magnitude *F*. The two spheres are then connected by a conducting wire, and then the wire is removed. In terms of *F*, the new force between them is

(A) zero
(B) 3*F*, attractive
(C) 2*F*, repulsive
(D) ½ *F*, attractive
(E) 1/3 *F*, repulsive

Questions 306–307

Four charges are arranged at the corners of a square of side *a* as shown.

306. Which of the following is true of the electric field and the electric potential at the center of the square?

	Electric Field	Electric Potential
(A)	zero	zero
(B)	$\dfrac{kQ}{a\sqrt{2}}$	zero
(C)	$\dfrac{kQ^2}{2a^2}$	$\dfrac{kQ}{2a}$
(D)	zero	$\dfrac{kQ}{\sqrt{2a}}$
(E)	$\dfrac{kQ^2}{2a}$	$\dfrac{kQ}{a\sqrt{2}}$

307. Which of the following diagrams best represents how you might rearrange the charges so that the electric field would point directly upward toward the top of the page?

(A)

(B)

(C)

(D)

(E)

308. Three charges, $+Q$, $-Q$, and $+2Q$, are arranged in an equilateral triangle as shown. Which of the arrows below best represents the direction of the electric field at the center of the triangle?

(A) ↓

(B) ↑

(C) ↘

(D) ↙

(E) ↗

Questions 309–310

A positive charge Q is placed on a spherical shell of radius R.

309. Which of the following graphs best represents the electric field E as a function of distance r from the center of the sphere?

(A)

(B)

(C)

(D)

(E)

310. Which of the following graphs best represents the electric potential V as a function of distance r from the center of the sphere?

(A)

(B)

(C)

(D)

(E)

Questions 311–312
A nonconducting sphere of uniform charge density ρ contains a total charge $+Q$.

311. Which of the following graphs best represents the electric field E as a function of distance r from the center of the sphere?

(A)

(B)

(C)

(D)

(E)

312. Which of the following graphs best represents the electric potential
V as a function of distance r from the center of the sphere?

(A)

(B)

(C)

(D)

(E)

Questions 313–314

A nonconducting sphere does not have a uniform charge density, but the density ρ varies with the distance r from the center of the sphere according to the equation $\rho = \beta r$, where β is a positive constant.

313. The electric field inside the sphere ($r < R$) at a distance r from the center of the sphere is

(A) $\dfrac{\beta r^2}{12\varepsilon_o}$

(B) $\dfrac{\beta r}{2\varepsilon_o}$

(C) $\dfrac{\beta r^3}{3\varepsilon_o}$

(D) $\dfrac{\beta r^2}{2\varepsilon_o}$

(E) $\dfrac{\beta r^2}{4\varepsilon_o}$

314. The electric potential at the surface of the sphere is

(A) $\dfrac{\beta R^3}{4\varepsilon_o}$

(B) $\dfrac{\beta R}{2\varepsilon_o}$

(C) $\dfrac{\beta R^3}{3\varepsilon_o}$

(D) $\dfrac{\beta R^2}{2\varepsilon_o}$

(E) $\dfrac{\beta R^2}{4\varepsilon_o}$

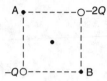

315. Two charges $-Q$ and $-2Q$ are located at the corners of a square of side a, as shown. Points A and B are at the opposite corners of the square. The work required to move a positive charge from point A to point B is

(A) negative
(B) positive
(C) dependent on the path from A to B
(D) equal to the electric potential between the charges
(E) zero

316. Two charges, $+4Q$ and $-Q$, are connected by an insulated rod and rest in a uniform electric field $\mathbf{E}$ as shown. Ignore the effects of gravity on the charges and rod. The rod and charges will experience

(A) a clockwise rotation and a downward acceleration
(B) a counterclockwise rotation and a downward acceleration
(C) a clockwise rotation and an upward acceleration
(D) a counterclockwise rotation and an upward acceleration
(E) no rotation, but a downward acceleration

Questions 317–318
A positive charge Q is placed at the center of a hollow conducting sphere.

317. The charge on the inside surface of the hollow sphere is

(A) $-Q$
(B) $+Q$
(C) $-2Q$
(D) $+2Q$
(E) zero

318. A grounding wire is connected to the sphere, and then removed. The charge on the sphere is now

(A) $-Q$
(B) $+Q$
(C) $-2Q$
(D) $+2Q$
(E) zero

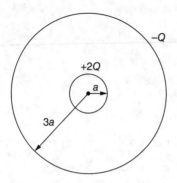

Questions 319–320

A solid conducting sphere of radius a is placed inside a conducting spherical shell of radius $3a$, as shown. A charge $+2Q$ is placed on the inner sphere, and a charge $-Q$ is placed on the outer sphere.

319. Which of the following graphs best represents the electric field E as a function of the distance r from the center of the spheres?

(A)

(B)

(C)

(D)

(E)

320. Which of the following graphs best represents the electric potential
V as a function of the distance *r* from the center of the spheres?

(A)

(B)

(C)

(D)

(E)

321. An irregularly shaped solid conductor has a positive charge placed
on its surface. Which of the following statements is true of the
conductor?

(A) The surface of the conductor is an equipotential surface.

(B) The electric field must be directed radially inward.

(C) The electric field is constant throughout the surface of the
conductor.

(D) The surface charge density is constant throughout the surface of
the conductor.

(E) Negative work is required to move a positive charge from one
side of the conductor to the other.

322. The potential V as a function of distance r for a particular charge distribution is given by the equation $V = ar^{-1}$. The electric field as a function of distance r from the charge distribution is

(A) $1/3\ ar^{-3}$
(B) $2ar^{-1}$
(C) ar^{-2}
(D) $-a(ln\ r)$
(E) $-ar^{-2}$

323. A positive charge of 4 μC is moved by an external force applied in the same direction as an electric field of magnitude 4000 N/C. If the charge is moved a distance of 0.2 m, the work done by the external force is

(A) 200 μJ
(B) 800 μJ
(C) 1600 μJ
(D) 3200 μJ
(E) 6400 μJ

Mass of oil droplet	3.2×10^{-7} kg
Charge on oil droplet	8.0×10^{-9} C
Electric field strength between the plates	200 N/C
Acceleration due to gravity	9.81 m/s^2

324. A charged oil droplet is located between two charged parallel plates as shown. The data table shows the measurements made by a student. Which of the following is true?

(A) The droplet will accelerate upward.
(B) The droplet will remain at rest.
(C) The droplet will move upward with a constant velocity.
(D) The droplet will move downward with a constant velocity.
(E) The droplet will accelerate downward.

325. Two conducting spheres, A and B, are separated by a large distance compared to their radii. Sphere A has a radius R, and sphere B has a radius $2R$. They each carry an equal charge $-Q$. The two spheres are then connected by a wire. In which direction will current flow in the wire?

(A) From A to B, since the potential is greater on the surface of sphere A.

(B) From B to A, since the potential is greater on the surface of sphere B.

(C) No current will flow between them, since the potential is the same for both spheres.

(D) No current will flow between them, since the charge is the same for both spheres.

(E) No current will flow between them, since the radius is not the same for both spheres.

Questions 326–327

A positively charged ring of radius R is made of conducting material and has a charge Q distributed uniformly around it. The center of the ring is located at point 0 on the x-axis.

326. The potential V at a distance $3d$ from point 0 on the x-axis is

(A) $V = \dfrac{kQ}{9d^2}$

(B) $V = \dfrac{kQ}{3d^2}$

(C) $V = \dfrac{kQ}{R^2 + 9d^2}$

(D) $V = \sqrt{\dfrac{kQ}{R^2 + 9d^2}}$

(E) $\dfrac{kQ}{\sqrt{R^2 + 9d^2}}$

327. Which of the following graphs best represents the electric field E as a function of distance along the x-axis?

(A)

(B)

(C)

(D)

(E)

328. According to Gauss's law, the net electric flux passing through a closed surface is

(A) positive if the flux is entering the surface
(B) negative if the flux is exiting the surface
(C) positive if the net charge inside the surface is zero
(D) negative if the net charge inside the surface is zero
(E) zero if the net charge inside the surface is zero

329. According to Gauss's law, which of the following statements is true?

(A) It is possible to have a nonzero electric field, but zero electric flux.
(B) It is possible to have a nonzero electric flux, but zero electric field.
(C) It is possible to have a nonzero electric flux through a closed surface even if the enclosed charge in a surface is zero.
(D) If a surface is not closed (such as a sheet of paper), the flux through it must be zero.
(E) It is possible for charges located outside a closed surface to produce a net positive flux through the surface.

330. Electric potential

(A) is a vector quantity that depends on the direction of the electric field
(B) is a scalar quantity that depends on the magnitude and sign of charges in the vicinity
(C) is a scalar quantity that depends on the square of the distance from the charges in the vicinity
(D) is a vector quantity that depends on the sign of the charges in the vicinity
(E) is a vector quantity that must point from high to low potential

Questions 331–332

The two conducting spheres shown each have a charge Q on their surfaces. The larger sphere has a radius $4R$, and the smaller sphere has a radius R. The two spheres are far enough apart that their electric fields do not affect each other.

331. The ratio of the electric field near the surface of the larger sphere to the electric field near the surface of the smaller sphere is

(A) 16
(B) 4
(C) 2
(D) ¼
(E) 1/16

332. The ratio of the electric potential near the surface of the larger sphere to the electric potential near the surface of the smaller sphere is

(A) 4
(B) 2
(C) 1
(D) ½
(E) ¼

333. Which of the following statements is true of electric field and equipotential lines?

(A) The electric field vector always points in the same direction as the equipotential lines.
(B) The electric field always points in the opposite direction of the equipotential lines.
(C) The electric field always points perpendicular to the equipotential lines.
(D) The electric field is always equal to the equipotential lines.
(E) Equipotential lines always form a circle around electric field lines.

334. Electric field lines generally point from

    (A) low potential to high potential
    (B) high potential to low potential
    (C) negative charges to positive charges
    (D) negative potential to positive potential
    (E) low charge density to high charge density

    +   +   +   +

    −   −   −   −

335. Two oppositely charged parallel plates are shown in the figure. Which of the following diagrams best represents the equipotential lines between the plates?

    (A)

    (B)

    (C)

    (D)

    (E)

Questions 336–337
A nonconducting spherical charge distribution has a nonuniform positive charge density ρ. The center of the sphere is point 0, the radius of the sphere is a. The sphere is centered on the x-axis. A point inside the sphere lies on the x-axis at a distance x_1 from the center of the sphere. Another point, x_2, is outside the sphere on the x-axis.

336. The electric field at point x_2 can be determined by

    (A) using Gauss's law to determine the electric field from 0 to a, then using Gauss's law to determine the electric field from a to x_2, then finding the difference between the two electric fields.

    (B) using Gauss's law to determine the electric field from 0 to a, then using Gauss's law to determine the electric field from a to x_2, then finding the sum of the two electric fields.

    (C) integrating the electric potential outside the sphere from infinity to a, then integrating the electric potential inside the sphere from a to x_1, then finding the difference between the two potential integrals.

    (D) integrating the electric potential outside the sphere from infinity to a, then integrating the electric potential inside the sphere from a to x_1, then finding the sum of the two potential integrals.

    (E) determining the derivative of the potential function inside and outside the sphere, then finding the difference between the two derivatives.

337. The electric potential at point x_1 can be determined by

   (A) determining the derivative of the electric field function inside and outside the sphere, then finding the difference between the two derivatives.

   (B) determining the derivative of the electric field function inside and outside the sphere, then finding the sum of the two derivatives.

   (C) integrating the derivative of the product of the electric field and potential functions, then finding their sum.

   (D) integrating the electric field outside the sphere from infinity to a, then integrating the electric field inside the sphere from a to x_1, then finding the sum of the two potentials.

   (E) integrating the electric field outside the sphere from infinity to a, then integrating the electric field inside the sphere from a to x_1, then finding the difference between the two potentials.

338. A simple electroscope consists of a metal knob at the top of a metal rod as shown. Two thin gold foil leaves hang at the bottom of the rod. The rod and leaves are in an insulated container. A positively charged rod is brought near but not touching the knob of the electroscope, and then a student touches the knob with her finger. Afterward, both the positive rod and her finger are removed. Which of the following statements is true after she removes the rod and her finger?

   (A) The knob is positively charged, and the leaves are negatively charged.

   (B) The knob is negatively charged, and the leaves are positively charged.

   (C) Both the knob and the leaves are negatively charged.

   (D) Both the knob and the leaves are positively charged.

   (E) Both the knob and the leaves are neutral.

Questions 339–340

A cube has sides of length a. The cube rests so that one side rests on the x-axis as shown. An electric field is established in the x-direction according to the function $E_x = bx^2$, where b is a positive constant.

339. Which of the following statements is true?

(A) There is a net charge inside the cube.

(B) There is no net charge inside the cube.

(C) The flux passing through the cube is negative.

(D) The flux passing through the cube is zero.

(E) The flux diminishes while passing through the cube.

340. The charge inside the cube can be expressed by the equation

(A) $\varepsilon_o ba$

(B) $\varepsilon_o ba^2$

(C) $\varepsilon_o ba^3$

(D) $\varepsilon_o ba^4$

(E) $\varepsilon_o b^2 a^2$

Questions 341–342

Two hollow coaxial cylinders are shown in the figure. The inner cylinder has a radius a and a charge $-Q$, and the outer cylinder has a radius b and a charge $+Q$. The length L of the cylinders is very long compared to the radii of the cylinders.

341. Point X is a distance r from the center of the cylinders. The electric field at point X outside the larger cylinder is

(A) $\dfrac{Q}{2\pi\varepsilon_o r_1 L}$

(B) $\dfrac{Q}{4\pi\varepsilon_o r_1 L}$

(C) $\dfrac{Q}{2\pi\varepsilon_o r_1^2 L}$

(D) $\dfrac{Q}{4\pi\varepsilon_o r_1^2 L}$

(E) zero

342. Point Y is halfway between the two cylinders at a distance of r_2 from the center of the cylinders. The electric field at r_2 is

(A) $\dfrac{Q}{2\pi\varepsilon_o r_2 L}$

(B) $\dfrac{Q}{4\pi\varepsilon_o r_2 L}$

(C) $\dfrac{Q}{2\pi\varepsilon_o r_2^2 L}$

(D) $\dfrac{Q}{4\pi\varepsilon_o r_2^2 L}$

(E) zero

343. Gauss's law is most convenient to use when calculating an electric field due to

(A) charges outside a closed surface
(B) charges inside a closed surface that has high symmetry
(C) charges inside a closed surface that has low symmetry
(D) a potential difference that is negative
(E) a potential difference that is positive

344. Gauss's law is convenient to use when the forces are produced by a distribution that

(A) is proportional to distance
(B) is negative
(C) follows the inverse square law
(D) is positive
(E) is described by a hyperbolic function

Free Response

Questions 345–347

Two equal positive point charges of magnitude q_1 and q_2 lie on a line as shown. The magnitude of the force between the charges in these locations is F.

345. At what location would q_1 have to be placed for the force to increase to $4F$?

346. At what location is the electric field zero?

347. At what location is the electric potential maximum?

Questions 348–350

Several point charges produce the equipotential lines shown.

348. At which point on the diagram is the magnitude of the electric field greatest? Explain.

349. Points C and D are approximately 0.02 m apart. Point F is halfway between points C and D. What is the electric field at point F?

350. A $+5.0 \ \mu C$ point charge is moved from point C to point E, then to point D by an external force. Determine the work done by the external force.

CHAPTER **8**

Electric Circuits,
Capacitors, Dielectrics

1.

2.

3.

4.

5.

351. Which pair of the resistor arrangements shown have the same resistance between points *a* and *b*?

(A) 1 and 2
(B) 2 and 3
(C) 3 and 4
(D) 4 and 5
(E) 1 and 5

Questions 352–353

352. What is the reading on the voltmeter if the battery has no internal resistance?

(A) 0.5 V
(B) 2 V
(C) 2.4 V
(D) 4.8 V
(E) 12 V

353. What is the reading on the ammeter if the battery has no internal resistance?

(A) 1 A
(B) 2 A
(C) 3 A
(D) 4 A
(E) 6 A

354. In the circuit shown, what effect would adding another resistor in parallel with the resistor labeled R have?

   (A) The reading on the voltmeter would increase.
   (B) The reading on the ammeter would increase.
   (C) The reading on the voltmeter would decrease.
   (D) The reading on the ammeter would decrease.
   (E) The reading on the ammeter would not change.

Questions 355–356
An adjustable resistor is connected to a battery of emf ε in a simple circuit. A graph of power vs. current in the battery is shown in the figure.

355. The emf ε of the battery is most nearly

   (A) 5 V
   (B) 10 V
   (C) 20 V
   (D) 40 V
   (E) 60 V

356. What is the resistance of the adjustable resistor when the power in the circuit is 10 watts?

(A) 1.25 Ω
(B) 1.5 Ω
(C) 2.5 Ω
(D) 5.0 Ω
(E) 10 Ω

357. Five resistors are made of the same material. Which of the following has the highest resistance?

(A)

(B)

(C)

(D)

(E)

I = 1A

3 Ω

12 V

r

2 Ω

2 Ω

358. The circuit shown has a battery of emf ε and an unknown internal resistance. The internal resistance of the battery is

(A) 1 Ω
(B) 2 Ω
(C) 3 Ω
(D) 4 Ω
(E) 5 Ω

359. The current flowing in a wire as a function of time is given by the equation $I = 4t^3$. The charge that passes through the wire from 0 s to 2 s is

(A) 2 C
(B) 4 C
(C) 8 C
(D) 16 C
(E) 24 C

6 V   2 Ω   1 A

a

b

360. A 6-V battery with an internal resistance produces 1 A of current in the part of the circuit shown. A voltmeter connected across the battery will read

(A) 2 V
(B) 4 V
(C) 6 V
(D) 8 V
(E) 12 V

361. Which of the following circuits dissipates the most power?

(A)

3 V   3 Ω

(B)

3 V   6 Ω

(C)

9 V   3 Ω

6 Ω

(D)

6 V   6 Ω   6 Ω

(E)

3 V   6 Ω   6 Ω

362. There are three batteries in the circuit shown. There may be other resistances not shown on the diagram. The potential difference between points *a* and *b* is

(A) 3 V
(B) 6 V
(C) 9 V
(D) 12 V
(E) 18 V

363. Several different resistors are connected to a constant voltage one at a time, and the power dissipated through each resistor is measured. Which of the following graphs best represents the power dissipated as a function of resistance?

(A)

(B)

(C)

(D)

(E)

364. Each resistance in the five circuits below has a value of 2 Ω. Each circuit is connected to a 6 V battery. Which of the circuits would dissipate 9 watts of power?

(A)

(B)

(C)

(D)

(E)

Questions 365–366

Four identical light bulbs are connected to a battery as shown.

365. Which bulb will burn the brightest?

(A) 1
(B) 2
(C) 3
(D) 4
(E) All will emit the same brightness.

366. If bulb 4 is removed, how will the brightness of each of the bulbs change, if at all?

(A) Bulb 2 will be less bright.
(B) Bulb 2 will be brighter.
(C) Bulb 3 will not change its brightness.
(D) Bulb 1 will not give off light.
(E) None of the bulbs will change their brightness.

367. Circuit I and Circuit II shown each consist of a capacitor and a resistor. A battery is connected across *a* and *b*, and then removed. Which of the following statements is true of the circuits?

(A) Circuit I and Circuit II will both retain stored energy when the battery is removed.

(B) Neither Circuit I nor Circuit II will retain stored energy when the battery is removed.

(C) Only Circuit I will retain stored energy when the battery is removed.

(D) Only Circuit II will retain stored energy when the battery is removed.

(E) Current will continue to flow in both circuits after the battery is removed.

368. A parallel-plate capacitor has a capacitance *C*. A second parallel-plate capacitor has 4 times the area of the first, but ½ the separation distance between the plates. The capacitance of the second capacitor is

(A) 1/8 *C*

(B) ¼ *C*

(C) 2 *C*

(D) 4 *C*

(E) 8 *C*

369. Two capacitors are connected in parallel. One of the capacitors has a capacitance C_o and the other has a capacitance $2C_o$. A voltage V is applied across the capacitors. What is the ratio of the stored charge on the larger capacitor $2C_o$ to the charge stored on the smaller capacitor $2C_o$?

(A) ¼
(B) ½
(C) 2
(D) 4
(E) 8

Questions 370–371
A circuit consisting of a battery and four capacitors is shown.

370. The equivalent capacitance of this circuit is
(A) $7/4\ \mu F$
(B) $4/7\ \mu F$
(C) $21/16\ \mu F$
(D) $10\ \mu F$
(E) $22\ \mu F$

371. The charge stored on the 2 μF capacitor is most nearly

(A) 6 μC

(B) 12 μC

(C) 22 μC

(D) 36 μC

(E) 120 μC

372. Kirchoff's junction rule states that the current entering a junction in a circuit must also exit that junction. This rule is an expression of

(A) conservation of charge

(B) conservation of energy

(C) Ohm's law

(D) Ampere's law

(E) Gauss's law

373. Two parallel conducting plates are connected to a battery and are separated by a distance d. If the separation distance is doubled to $2d$ while the battery remains connected to the plates, which of the following will occur?

(A) The capacitance is doubled.

(B) The charge on the plates is doubled.

(C) The voltage across the plates is doubled.

(D) The electric field between the plates is halved.

(E) The capacitance does not change.

374. A 10 μF capacitor is connected to a 12 V battery. The energy stored in the capacitor is

(A) 120 μJ

(B) 540 μJ

(C) 600 μJ

(D) 720 μJ

(E) 1440 μJ

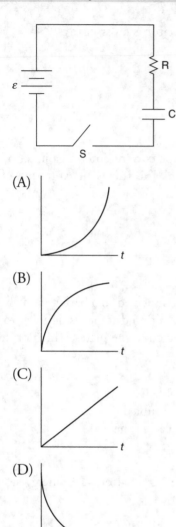

(A)

(B)

(C)

(D)

(E)

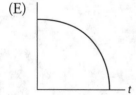

Questions 375–377

The capacitor in the circuit shown is initially uncharged when the switch S is closed at time $t = 0$. The graphs below could represent several quantities as a function of time for the circuit after the switch is closed.

375. Which of the graphs best represents the current in the circuit as a function of time?

(A) A
(B) B
(C) C
(D) D
(E) E

376. Which of the graphs best represents the voltage across the resistor as a function of time?

(A) A
(B) B
(C) C
(D) D
(E) E

377. Which of the graphs best represents the voltage across the capacitor as a function of time?

(A) A
(B) B
(C) C
(D) D
(E) E

378. Three 10 μF capacitors are connected in parallel with a 10-volt battery. The equivalent capacitance of the circuit is

(A) 3.3 μF
(B) 5 μF
(C) 10 μF
(D) 20 μF
(E) 30 μF

379. Three 9 μF capacitors are connected in series with a 9-volt battery. The charge on each capacitor is

(A) 1 μC
(B) 3 μC
(C) 6 μC
(D) 9 μC
(E) 27 μC

380. Three 6 μF capacitors are connected in series with a 6-volt battery. The energy stored on each capacitor is

(A) 1 μJ
(B) 3 μJ
(C) 4 μJ
(D) 6 μJ
(E) 12 μJ

381. A capacitor C_o is connected to a battery and stores charge. If the space between the capacitor plates is filled with oil, which of the following quantities increase?

(A) Capacitance and voltage across the plates
(B) Charge and voltage across the plates
(C) Capacitance and electric field between the plates
(D) Capacitance and charge on the plates
(E) Electric field between the plates and voltage across the plates

Questions 382–384

The circuit shows a capacitor, a battery, and a resistor. Switch S is first connected to point a to charge the capacitor, then a long time later switched to point b to discharge the capacitor through the resistor.

382. The time constant τ for discharging the capacitor through the resistor could be decreased (faster discharge) by

(A) placing another resistor in series with the first resistor
(B) placing another resistor in parallel with the first resistor
(C) placing another capacitor in parallel with the first capacitor
(D) placing another battery in series in the same direction with the first battery
(E) increasing both R and C

383. The maximum current through the resistor is

(A) $\varepsilon/2R$
(B) ε/R
(C) ε/RC
(D) $\varepsilon/2RC$
(E) $C\varepsilon/R$

384. Which of the graphs below best represents the current through the resistor as a function of time for a full charging and discharging cycle?

(A)

(B)

(C)

(D)

(E)

Questions 385–386

The equation for determining the capacitance of a capacitor of plate area A and separation d is $C = \dfrac{\varepsilon_o A}{d}$.

385. This equation can be derived from

(A) Ampere's law
(B) Faraday's law of induction
(C) Gauss's law for electrostatics
(D) Gauss's law for magnetism
(E) Ohm's law of circuits

386. If a dielectric of constant $\kappa = 4$ is placed between the plates of the capacitor and the separation between the plates is decreased to ½ d, the capacitance

(A) increases by a factor of 4
(B) decreases by a factor of 4
(C) increases by a factor of 8
(D) decreases by a factor of 8
(E) is unchanged

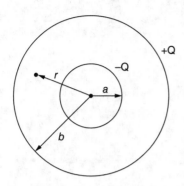

Questions 387–389

The spherical capacitor shown consists of a conducting shell of radius a inside a larger conducting shell of radius b. A charge $-Q$ is placed on the inner sphere and a charge $+Q$ is placed on the outer shell. The capacitance of the capacitor is C_o.

387. The magnitude of the electric field E at a distance r between the spheres is

(A) $\dfrac{Q}{4\pi\varepsilon_o r^2}$

(B) $\dfrac{Q}{4\pi\varepsilon_o r}$

(C) $\dfrac{Q}{4\pi\varepsilon_o a^2}$

(D) $\dfrac{Q}{4\pi\varepsilon_o b^2}$

(E) zero

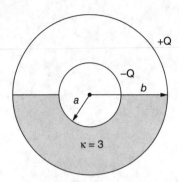

388. The bottom half of the space between the spheres is filled with oil of dielectric constant $\kappa = 3$, creating two capacitors connected to each other. Which of the following is true of the two capacitors?

(A) They are connected in series.
(B) They are connected in parallel.
(C) The total capacitance has not changed.
(D) The total capacitance of the spheres has decreased.
(E) The total capacitance is now zero.

389. With the bottom half of the space between the spheres having been filled with oil of dielectric constant $\kappa = 3$, the new capacitance of the spheres is

(A) zero
(B) C_o
(C) $2C_o$
(D) $3C_o$
(E) $4C_o$

Questions 390–392

The cylindrical capacitor shown consists of a conducting shell of radius a inside a larger conducting shell of radius b. A charge $-Q$ is placed on the inner sphere and a charge $+Q$ is placed on the outer shell. The length of the capacitor is L, which is very long compared to a and b. The capacitance of the capacitor is C_0.

390. The magnitude of the electric field E at a distance r between the cylinders is

(A) $\dfrac{Q}{4\pi\varepsilon_0 r^2}$

(B) $\dfrac{Q}{\pi\varepsilon_0 rL}$

(C) $\dfrac{Q}{2\pi\varepsilon_0 rL}$

(D) $\dfrac{Q}{2\pi\varepsilon_0 L^2}$

(E) zero

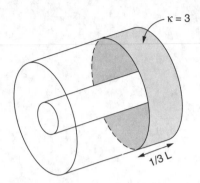

391. One-third of the length of the space between the cylinders is filled with oil of dielectric constant $\kappa = 3$, creating two capacitors connected to each other. Which of the following is true of the two capacitors?

(A) They are connected in series.
(B) They are connected in parallel.
(C) The total capacitance has not changed.
(D) The total capacitance of the spheres has decreased.
(E) The total capacitance is now zero.

392. With one-third of the space between the cylinders having been filled with oil of dielectric constant $\kappa = 3$, the new capacitance of the spheres is

(A) zero
(B) C_o
(C) $1/3\ C_o$
(D) $5/3\ C_o$
(E) $4C_o$

393. A battery of voltage V_o is attached to two parallel conducting plates. Charge is distributed on the plates, and then the battery is removed. A dielectric is then inserted between the plates, filling the space. Which of the following decreases after the battery is removed and the dielectric is inserted to fill the space between the plates?

(A) Capacitance
(B) Charge on the plates
(C) Net electric field between the plates
(D) Area of the plates
(E) Separation distance between the plates

Free Response

Questions 394–396

The circuit shown includes an unknown resistance R. The current in the circuit is 2 A.

394. What is the value of the resistance R?

395. What will a voltmeter read if it is connected from point a to point b?

396. How much energy is dissipated in the 1.0 Ω resistor in a time of 30 s?

Questions 397–400

A capacitor C is fully charged when it is connected in a circuit to a resistance R. As the capacitor discharges, the equation for the charge q on the capacitor as a function of time t is $(t) = 6e^{\frac{-t}{4}}$, where charge is in coulombs.

397. What is the maximum charge on the capacitor before discharging?

398. Write an expression for current as a function of time as the capacitor discharges.

399. What does the number 4 in the denominator of the exponent of e represent?

400. Show that the product of resistance and capacitance has the SI units of time.

CHAPTER 9

Magnetic Fields and Forces

401. A straight wire carries a current I as shown. The magnetic field **B** at a point a distance r above the wire is

(A) $2\pi r I$ directed into the page

(B) $\mu_o I$ directed out of the page

(C) $\dfrac{\mu_o I}{2\pi r}$ directed into the page

(D) $\dfrac{\mu_o I}{2\pi r}$ directed out of the page

(E) zero

Questions 402–403

Two wires carry currents 2A and 4A in the directions shown. Point P is a distance r from the wire carrying 2A, and a distance $2r$ from the wire carrying 4A.

402. Which of the following statements is true?

(A) The magnetic field produced at point P by the wire carrying 2A is greater than the magnetic field produced at point P by the wire carrying 4A, but opposite in direction.

(B) The magnetic field produced at point P by the wire carrying 2A is less than the magnetic field produced at point P by the wire carrying 4A, and in the same direction.

(C) The magnetic field produced at point P by the wire carrying 2A is equal to the magnetic field produced at point P by the wire carrying 4A, but opposite in direction.

(D) The magnetic field produced at point P by the wire carrying 2A is equal to the magnetic field produced at point P by the wire carrying 4A, and in the same direction.

(E) The magnetic field produced at point P by the wire carrying 2A is greater than the magnetic field produced at point P by the wire carrying 4A, and in the same direction.

403. The magnitude of the resultant magnetic field at point P due to the current in the two wires is

(A) zero

(B) $\dfrac{\mu_o(2A)}{2\pi r}$

(C) $\dfrac{\mu_o(2A)}{\pi r}$

(D) $\dfrac{\mu_o(4A)}{2\pi r}$

(E) $\dfrac{\mu_o(6A)}{4\pi r}$

Questions 404–405

Two wires are parallel to each other, one carrying twice the current as the other. The two currents flow in the same direction.

404. Which of the following is true of the forces the wires exert on each other?

(A) The wire with the larger current exerts a greater force on the other wire.

(B) The wire with the smaller current exerts a greater force on the other wire.

(C) The wires exert equal and opposite forces on each other.

(D) The wires exert equal forces on each other, but in the same direction.

(E) The net force between the wires is zero.

405. The direction of the force between the wires is

(A) repulsive

(B) attractive

(C) zero

(D) into the page

(E) out of the page

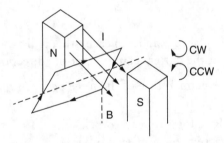

406. An electric motor consists of a current-carrying loop of wire mounted to an axle and turned at a slight angle in a magnetic field as shown. The wire loop will

(A) experience a torque and turn clockwise

(B) experience a torque and turn counterclockwise

(C) accelerate upward out of the magnetic field

(D) accelerate downward out of the magnetic field

(E) not experience a force or torque

407. A current is passed through an analog ammeter and the needle moves to indicate the current flowing through the circuit. Which of the following best explains how an analog ammeter works?

(A) Current is passed through the needle placed in a magnetic field, and the needle is attracted to the high side of the scale.

(B) The needle is a magnet, and is attracted to a magnet on the high side of the scale.

(C) The needle gathers an electrostatic charge from the current, and is attracted to an electrostatic charge on the high side of the scale.

(D) Current is passed through a spring coil of wire placed in a magnetic field, and the coil rotates, moving the needle proportionally to the current in the coil.

(E) Current flows through the needle, making it heavier, and it falls to the high side of the scale.

Questions 408–410

Two wire loops of equal radius are placed parallel to each other a distance d apart. Each carries a current I_o, but the currents are in opposite directions.

408. Which of the following statements is true of the force between the loops?

(A) The loops exert a repulsive force on each other.

(B) The loops exert an attractive force on each other.

(C) The loops exert a force on each other in such a way that they will accelerate up toward the top of the page.

(D) The loops exert a force on each other in such a way that they will accelerate down toward the bottom of the page.

(E) The loops do not apply a force to each other.

409. Which of the following could be done to increase the force between the loops by a factor of 4?

(A) Double the current in one of the loops
(B) Reduce the current in one loop by half
(C) Reduce the current in both loops by half
(D) Double the distance between them
(E) Double the current in both of the loops

410. The direction of the net magnetic field at the center of the loop on the right is

(A) directed into the page
(B) directed out of the page
(C) directed to the right
(D) directed to the left
(E) zero

411. A wire in the plane of the page carries a current directed to the right as shown. The wire is placed in a magnetic field that is directed into the plane of the page. The force the magnetic field applies to the wire is

(A) directed into the page
(B) directed out of the page
(C) directed to the top of the page
(D) directed to the bottom of the page
(E) zero

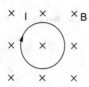

412. A loop of wire in the plane of the page carries a clockwise current I and is placed in a magnetic field that is directed into the page as shown. Which of the following will happen as a result of the wire loop being in the magnetic field?

(A) The wire loop will rotate clockwise.
(B) The wire loop will rotate counterclockwise.
(C) The wire loop will flip on a horizontal axis through its center.
(D) The wire loop will expand in size.
(E) The wire loop will contract in size.

Questions 413–414

Two long parallel wires are separated by a distance $2d$ as shown. Each wire carries a current I, both directed into the page. Point P lies halfway between the two wires on the x-axis, and point N lies a distance d on the y-axis.

413. The resultant magnetic field at point P is

(A) zero

(B) $\dfrac{\mu_o I}{2\pi d}$

(C) $\dfrac{\mu_o I}{\pi d}$

(D) $\dfrac{\mu_o (2I)}{\pi d}$

(E) $\dfrac{\mu_o I}{2\pi d^2}$

414. The direction of the resultant magnetic field at point N is best represented by which of the arrows below?

(A) ↓

(B) ↑

(C) ↘

(D) ←

(E) →

Questions 415–417
An electron enters a magnetic field that is directed out of the page as shown. The velocity of the electron is to the right.

415. The force the magnetic field exerts on the electron when it enters the magnetic field is

(A) directed into the page

(B) directed out of the page

(C) directed to the top of the page

(D) directed to the bottom of the page

(E) zero

416. The resulting path of the electron after entering the magnetic field is a

(A) straight line

(B) circle

(C) spiral

(D) parabola

(E) hyperbola

417. The work done by the magnetic field on the electron for one complete revolution at a radius r is

(A) $qvBr$

(B) qvB/r

(C) qv/Br

(D) Br/qv

(E) zero

Questions 418–419

The velocity **v** of a positive charge is directed out of the page as shown, and experiences a magnetic force **F** at an angle to the horizontal due to traveling through a magnetic field **B**.

418. Which of the arrows below best represents the direction of the magnetic field **B** that applies the force **F** to the positive charge?

(A) ↓

(B) ↑

(C) ↘

(D) ↖

(E) →

419. The magnetic field is rotated so that the angle between the velocity **v** and the magnetic field **B** is 30°. The resulting path of the electron in this magnetic field is a

(A) straight line

(B) circle

(C) spiral

(D) parabola

(E) hyperbola

420. Two wires, 1 and 2, are separated by a distance d as shown. Point M is located at a distance d above wire 1. When there is only current flowing in wire 1 and none in wire 2, the magnitude of the magnetic field at point M is B_1. If a current is established in wire 2 so that both wires now have equal currents I, with both directed to the right, the magnetic field at point M is

(A) ½ B_1
(B) 2/3 B_1
(C) ¾ B_1
(D) 3/2 B_1
(E) zero

Questions 421–422
A positive charge $q = 2 \times 10^{-6}$ C enters a region of magnetic field $B = 0.2$ T directed into the page with a speed $v = 2 \times 10^6$ m/s directed down to the bottom of the page.

421. The magnitude and direction of the magnetic force acting on the positive charge is

(A) 0.2 N to the right
(B) 0.4 N to the left
(C) 0.8 N to the right
(D) 1.0 N to the left
(E) 4.0 N to the right

422. An electric field E is established in the same region as the magnetic field just as the positive charge enters the region. The direction of the electric field that would keep the charge moving in a straight line is best represented by which of the arrows below?

(A) ↓

(B) ↑

(C) ↘

(D) ←

(E) →

Questions 423–424

A negative charge $q = 4 \times 10^{-6}$ C enters a region of magnetic field $B = 0.5$ T directed into the page with a speed $v = 8 \times 10^6$ m/s directed to the right. An electric field also exists in the same region, causing the negative charge to follow a straight path.

423. Which of the following arrows best represents the direction of the electric field?

(A) ↓

(B) ↑

(C) ↘

(D) ←

(E) →

424. The magnitude of the electric field E that would cause the negative charge to follow a straight path is

(A) 2×10^6 N/C

(B) 4×10^6 N/C

(C) 8×10^6 N/C

(D) 2×10^7 N/C

(E) 4×10^7 N/C

425. A thin sheet of copper is placed in a uniform magnetic field. A battery is connected to the top and bottom ends of the copper sheet, so that conventional current flows from the top to the bottom of the sheet. Points X and Y are on the left and right sides of the sheet, respectively. Which of the following statements is true?

(A) Point X is at a higher potential than point Y.
(B) Point Y is at a higher potential than point X.
(C) Point X and point Y are at equal potential.
(D) Point X is at zero potential, and point Y has a positive potential.
(E) Point Y is at zero potential, and point X has a negative potential.

Questions 426–427
A wire carries a current I. Point P is a perpendicular distance r from the wire. An imaginary circle of radius r is drawn around the wire.

426. Which of the following is a correct application of Ampere's law that can be used to solve for the magnetic field B at point P?

(A) $\dfrac{B}{2\pi r} = \mu_o I$

(B) $\dfrac{B}{4\pi r^2} = \mu_o I$

(C) $B(2\pi r) = \mu_o I$

(D) $B(\pi r^2) = \mu_o I$

(E) $\dfrac{B}{2\pi r} = \dfrac{\mu_o I}{2r}$

427. Which of the graphs below best represents the magnetic field B as a function of distance from the wire r?

(A)

(B)

(C)

(D)

(E)

Questions 428–430

A cross section of a solenoid of length L and radius r is shown. A current I is passed through the solenoid so that the current comes out toward you on the bottom and into the page on the top. An imaginary square of side x is drawn on the figure.

428. The magnetic field in the region just outside the solenoid at a distance d from the center of the solenoid is

 (A) zero

 (B) $\dfrac{\mu_o I}{2\pi d}$

 (C) $\dfrac{\mu_o I}{\pi d}$

 (D) $\dfrac{\mu_o (2I)}{\pi d}$

 (E) $\dfrac{\mu_o I}{2\pi d^2}$

429. The direction of the magnetic field inside the solenoid is best represented by which of the arrows below?

 (A) ↓

 (B) ↑

 (C) ↘

 (D) ←

 (E) →

430. Ampere's law can correctly be applied to the imaginary square path *abcd* to determine the magnetic field produced by the solenoid in which of the following equations?

(A) $\int_{c}^{d} B \cdot dl = \mu_o I$

(B) $\int_{a}^{b} B \cdot dl = \mu_o I_{enc}$

(C) $\int_{b}^{c} B \cdot dl = \mu_o I_{enc}$

(D) $\int_{a}^{a} B \cdot dl = \mu_o I_{enc}$

(E) $\int_{b}^{b} B \cdot dl = \mu_o I_{enc}$

Questions 431–433

A negatively charged particle of mass *m* and charge *q* in a uniform magnetic field *B* travels in a circular path of radius *r*.

431. In terms of the other given quantities, the charge-to-mass ratio q/m of the particle is

(A) $\dfrac{Bv}{r}$

(B) $\dfrac{r}{Bv}$

(C) $\dfrac{rv}{B}$

(D) rvB

(E) $\dfrac{v}{rB}$

432. The work done by the magnetic field after two full revolutions of the charge is

(A) zero
(B) $-qvB/rm$
(C) qvm/Br
(D) $-mBr/qv$
(E) $-mqvBr$

433. Which of the following graphs best represents the radius r as a function of magnetic field B for a constant speed?

(A)

(B)

(C)

(D)

(E)

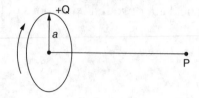

Questions 434–436

A ring of radius *r* has a positive charge +*Q* distributed uniformly around its circumference. The ring begins to rotate clockwise about the *x*-axis with a constant speed *v*, with the charge *Q* rotating with the ring. The period of rotation is *T*. Point P is on the *x*-axis a distance *d* from the center of the ring.

434. The current produced by the rotation is

(A) $\dfrac{Q}{2\pi T}$

(B) $\dfrac{Q}{2\pi r T}$

(C) $\dfrac{2\pi r}{T}$

(D) $\dfrac{Q}{T}$

(E) zero

435. The direction of the magnetic field at the center of the loop is

(A) ↓

(B) ↑

(C) ↘

(D) ←

(E) →

436. The direction of the magnetic field at point P due to the rotating ring is

(A) ↓

(B) ↑

(C) ↘

(D) ←

(E) →

Questions 437–439

A very long conducting slab of copper of height a and width b carries a current I throughout its cross-sectional area. The current density j is constant throughout the slab, and is directed out of the page through the facing area of the slab. Points X and Y are marked on the facing area of the slab.

437. The current density j can be expressed by the expression

    (A) $\dfrac{I}{a^2}$

    (B) $\dfrac{I}{b^2}$

    (C) $\dfrac{I}{(ab)^2}$

    (D) $\dfrac{I}{ab}$

    (E) $\dfrac{I}{a+b}$

438. Which of the following diagrams best represents the integration path taken to apply Ampere's law to determine the magnetic field at points X or Y inside the slab?

(A)

(B)

(C)

(D)

(E)

439. Which of the following best represents the direction of the magnetic field vectors at points X and Y?

(A)   X
      •⟶

      ⟵•
       Y

(B)   X
      ⟵•

      •⟶
       Y

(C)   X
      ↙•

      ↗•
      Y

(D)   X
      •↘

      ↖•
       Y

(E)   ↑
      •X

      •Y
      ↓

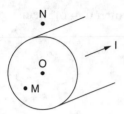

Questions 440–441

A long cylinder made of conducting material carries a total current I parallel to the length of the cylinder and directed into the page, as shown. The current density is uniform throughout the cross-sectional area of the cylinder. Point M is inside the cylinder and point N is outside the cylinder in the positions shown.

440. Which of the following arrows best represents the direction of the magnetic field vector at point M?

(A) ↓

(B) ↑

(C) ↘

(D) ↖

(E) →

441. Which of the following arrows best represents the direction of the magnetic field vector at point N?

(A) ↓

(B) ↑

(C) ↘

(D) ←

(E) →

Questions 442–443

A long coaxial cable consists of a solid cylindrical conductor of radius *a* surrounded by a hollow coaxial conductor of inner radius *b* and outer radius c. The two conductors each carry a uniformly distributed current *I*, but in opposite directions. Point P is outside the larger cylinder at a distance *d* from the center of the cylinders.

442. The magnetic field *B* at point P is

(A) zero

(B) $\dfrac{\mu_o I}{2\pi d}$

(C) $\dfrac{\mu_o I}{\pi d}$

(D) $\dfrac{\mu_o (2I)}{\pi d}$

(E) $\dfrac{\mu_o I}{2\pi d^2}$

443. Which of the graphs below best represents the magnetic field B as a function of distance from the center r?

(A)

(B)

(C)

(D)

(E)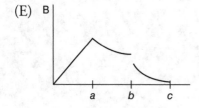

444. A stationary compass placed above a charge moving with a speed v deflects its needle so that it aligns perpendicular to the velocity of the charge. If the compass also moves at the speed v along with the charge, the compass will

(A) deflect 90° relative to the velocity of the charge
(B) deflect 60° relative to the velocity of the charge
(C) deflect 45° relative to the velocity of the charge
(D) deflect 180° relative to the velocity of the charge
(E) not deflect

Free Response

Questions 445–447
A solid conducting cylinder of radius a has a current I distributed uniformly throughout its cross-sectional area as shown.

445. Determine the magnetic field at a distance r greater than a.

446. Determine the magnetic field at a distance r less than a.

447. On the axes below, sketch the graph that best represents the magnetic field B as a function of distance r from the center of the cylinder.

Questions 448–450

An electron of mass m and charge q is accelerated from rest through a potential difference V toward a positively charged plate. The electron has a speed v when it enters a magnetic field B directed out of the page in the region just beyond the positive plate.

448. What is the potential difference V necessary to give the electron a speed v as it reaches the positive plate?

449. On the diagram above, sketch the path that best indicates the electron's motion in the magnetic field.

450. Determine the radius of orbit for the electron.

CHAPTER 10

Electromagnetic Induction, Inductance, and Maxwell's Equations

451. Which of the following will induce a current in a loop of wire?

(A) A magnetic field passes through the loop.
(B) A magnetic flux passes through the loop.
(C) A magnetic field is created outside the loop.
(D) A magnetic flux is changing through the loop.
(E) A magnetic flux is greater than the loop.

Questions 452–453

A rectangular loop of wire of width w and length L has a resistance R, and lies in the plane of the page. A magnetic field of strength B is directed out of the page as shown. The loop of wire moves to the right with a constant speed v.

452. What is the induced current in the loop?

(A) BLv/R^2
(B) BLv/wR^2
(C) $BLwv/R$
(D) BLv/R
(E) zero

453. The direction of the induced current in the loop is

    (A) out of the page

    (B) into the page

    (C) clockwise

    (D) counterclockwise

    (E) no direction, since the induced current is zero

454. In each of the diagrams below, a bar magnet and a loop of wire are aligned so that the magnet can pass through the loop. Which of the following situations would NOT induce a current in the loop?

(A)

(B)

(C)

(D)

(E)

Questions 455–456

A square loop of conducting wire lies in a plane that is perpendicular to a magnetic field $B = 0.3$ T, which is directed into the page. The square has an area of 0.4 m², and is turned a quarter of a turn in a time of 0.2 s in such a way that it becomes parallel to the magnetic field lines (that is, the magnetic field lines no longer pass through the loop).

455. During the quarter turn, the change in magnetic flux through the loop is

(A) 0.006 T m²
(B) 0.012 T m²
(C) 0.024 T m²
(D) 0.036 T m²
(E) 0.048 T m²

456. The average emf ε induced in the loop during the quarter turn is

(A) 0.006 V
(B) 0.012 V
(C) 0.024 V
(D) 0.036 V
(E) 0.048 V

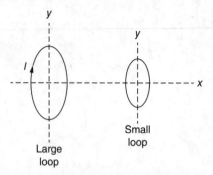

457. A large wire loop and a small wire loop are parallel to each other and centered on the x-axis as shown. The large loop carries a current *I*. Which of the following procedures will NOT induce a current in the smaller loop?

    (A) Changing the current in the larger loop at a constant rate
    (B) Rotating the smaller loop about the *y*-axis
    (C) Moving the larger loop toward the smaller loop at a constant velocity
    (D) Increasing the area of the smaller loop during a time interval
    (E) Rotating the smaller loop about the *x*-axis

458. A magnetic field directed into the page increases at a constant rate. The changing magnetic field passes perpendicularly through a wire loop of radius *r*. Which of the following statements is true of the induced current in the loop?

    (A) The induced current in the loop is zero.
    (B) The induced current in the loop is clockwise.
    (C) The induced current in the loop is counterclockwise.
    (D) The induced current in the loop is directed out of the page.
    (E) The induced current in the loop is directed into the page.

459. A thick wire of length L falls perpendicularly through a magnetic field that is directed out of the page. Which of the following graphs best represents the induced potential difference across the ends of the wire as a function of falling velocity?

(A)

(B)

(C)

(D)

(E)

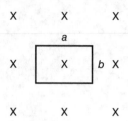

460. A rectangular loop of wire has a length a and width b and rests in a magnetic field that is directed into the page as shown. The resistance of the wire is R. The magnetic field is constantly changed so as to induce a current in the loop. The rate at which the magnetic field must change to produce the current I can be expressed as

(A) $\dfrac{Iab}{R}$

(B) $\dfrac{Ia}{bR}$

(C) $\dfrac{IR}{ab}$

(D) $\dfrac{ab}{IR}$

(E) $\dfrac{Ib}{bR}$

Questions 461–463

The top view of rails of width L is shown. A bar of length L lies perpendicular to the rails and slides without friction with a speed v. A magnetic field B is directed into the page throughout the area of the rails.

461. The direction of the induced current in the bar is

(A) to the left

(B) to the right

(C) into the page

(D) out of the page

(E) zero

462. The magnetic force **F** acting on the bar as it slides is

(A) $\dfrac{BLv}{R}$

(B) $\dfrac{BL^2v}{R}$

(C) $\dfrac{B^2L^2v}{R}$

(D) $\dfrac{B^2L^2v}{R^2}$

(E) zero

Questions 463–464

A rectangular loop of wire of length L and width w is mounted on a frictionless cart and passes through a constant magnetic field B with a speed v. The magnetic field is directed into the page and exists in a region with a width $2w$.

463. Which of the following graphs best represents the magnetic flux Φ through the loop as a function of distance x?

(A)

(B)

(C)

(D) Φ

(E) Φ

464. In reality, the speed of the loop may not remain constant. Which of the following statements is true of the speed of the loop as it passes through the magnetic field?

(A) The speed will decrease due to a negative magnetic force acting on the bar.

(B) The speed will increase due to a positive magnetic force acting on the bar.

(C) The speed will decrease because the magnetic flux is increasing.

(D) The speed will increase because the magnetic flux is decreasing.

(E) The speed of the bar will not change.

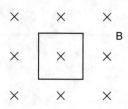

465. A square loop of side 0.2 m and resistance 0.5 Ω is placed in a magnetic field of 0.1 T directed into the page. The magnetic field decreases to zero at a constant rate during a time of 4 s. The magnitude and direction of the induced current in the loop is

(A) 0.0004 A
(B) 0.004 A
(C) 0.002 A
(D) 0.05 A
(E) 0.15 A

466. The north pole of a bar magnet is pushed through a conducting loop of wire so that it just crosses the plane of the loop, then is pulled back out of the loop. The current induced in the wire passing through point P at the top of the loop is

(A) first into the page away from you, then out of the page toward you

(B) first out of the page toward you, then into the page away from you

(C) down toward the bottom of the page, then up toward the top of the page

(D) up toward the top of the page, then down toward the bottom of the page

(E) always in the same direction as the motion of the magnet

Questions 467–470

A bar of mass 0.2 kg and length $L = 0.3$ m slides down a ramp made of two frictionless rails. The ramp forms an angle of 30° with the horizontal.

467. The acceleration of the bar as it slides down the ramp is most nearly

(A) zero
(B) 2 m/s^2
(C) 5 m/s^2
(D) 7 m/s^2
(E) 10 m/s^2

A magnetic field $B = 0.3$ T is established in a direction that passes through the rails perpendicularly to the plane of the ramp as shown. A current is induced in the bar as it slides down the rails.

468. Which of the following statements is true regarding the forces and motion involved?

(A) The only force acting on the bar as it slides is gravity.
(B) The only force acting on the bar as it slides is a magnetic force.
(C) Both a magnetic force and a component of the gravitational force act on the bar as it slides down the rails.
(D) The magnetic field changes as the bar slides down the rails.
(E) The magnetic flux is constant as the bar slides down the rails.

469. The current in the bar when the bar has reached its constant final speed is most nearly

(A) 1 A

(B) 2 A

(C) 3 A

(D) 5 A

(E) 10 A

470. The bar in the previous questions is now at rest at the bottom of the rails. The same magnetic field is now rotated so that it is directed straight downward toward the bottom of the page through the circuit formed by the rails and bar. The total length of the rails is 0.6 m. The magnetic flux Φ through the ramp surface is most nearly

(A) 0.078 T m^2

(B) 0.099 T m^2

(C) 0.11 T m^2

(D) 0.18 T m^2

(E) zero

Questions 471–472

A square conducting loop of wire of side s and resistance R is placed in a magnetic field B, which is directed out of the page as shown. The field increases with time t according to the equation $B = k + Ct$, where k and C are positive constants.

471. The rate of change of magnetic flux with respect to time is

(A) $s(k + Ct)$

(B) $s^2(k + Ct)$

(C) $s^2(Ct)$

(D) s^2C

(E) $2sk$

472. The induced current I in the square loop is

(A) $s(k + Ct)/R$
(B) $s^2(k + Ct)/R$
(C) $s^2(Ct)/R$
(D) s^2C/R
(E) $2sk/R$

473. A loop of wire is connected to a battery and carries a current I, as shown in the figure. The north pole of a magnet is placed near the center of the loop. The force the magnet applies to the current loop is

(A) zero
(B) directed up toward the top of the page
(C) directed down toward the bottom of the page
(D) directed out of the page
(E) directed into the page

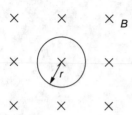

474. A circular loop of wire of radius r is placed in a magnetic field B that is varying with time. The induced emf ε in the loop is given by the equation $\varepsilon = k\pi r^2 t^{3/2}$, where k is a positive constant. The magnetic field B can be expressed as

(A) $\dfrac{3}{2}kt^{\frac{1}{2}}$

(B) $\dfrac{3}{2}kt^{\frac{3}{2}}$

(C) $\dfrac{2}{3}kt^{\frac{3}{2}}$

(D) $\dfrac{2}{3}kt^{\frac{5}{2}}$

(E) $\dfrac{4}{3}kt^{\frac{3}{2}}$

475. A mass m is attached to the bottom of a square conducting loop of side a as shown. The mass of the loop is negligible. The loop carries a current that causes the loop and mass to be suspended vertically in a magnetic field B, which is directed out of the page. The amount of current necessary to keep the loop and mass suspended in the field is

(A) $\dfrac{mg}{aB}$

(B) $\dfrac{aB}{mg}$

(C) $\dfrac{mg}{a^2B}$

(D) $\dfrac{a^2B}{mg}$

(E) $\dfrac{mg}{B}$

Questions 476–477

A magnetic field occupies a circular region of space of radius r. A conducting circular loop of wire of radius b and resistance R is placed in the magnetic field, which is directed out of the page as shown. The field decreases with time t according to the equation $B = B_0 - kt$, where k is a positive constant.

476. The magnitude of the current induced in the loop of wire is

(A) $\dfrac{b\pi r^2}{R}$

(B) $\dfrac{k\pi r^2}{R}$

(C) $\dfrac{\pi b^3}{R}$

(D) $\dfrac{\pi b^2}{R}$

(E) zero

477. The induced electric field E at the radius b is

(A) $\dfrac{kb^2}{2}$

(B) $\dfrac{kb}{2}$

(C) $\dfrac{kb^2}{2\pi}$

(D) $\dfrac{kb}{2\pi}$

(E) zero

Questions 478–479

A conducting loop of wire of area A is placed so that its plane is perpendicular to a magnetic field B. The magnetic field decreases according to the equation $B = 4e^{-2t}$.

478. The magnetic flux Φ as a function of time t is

(A) $4Ae^{-3t}$

(B) $8Ae^{-t}$

(C) $4Ae^{-2t}$

(D) $16Ae^{-2t}$

(E) $16Ae^{-4t}$

479. The induced current in the loop is

(A) $\dfrac{4Ae^{-3t}}{R}$

(B) $\dfrac{8Ae^{-t}}{R}$

(C) $\dfrac{8Ae^{-2t}}{R}$

(D) $\dfrac{16Ae^{-2t}}{R}$

(E) $\dfrac{16Ae^{-4t}}{R}$

480. Which of the following expressions could be used to determine the energy dissipated through the loop from $t = 0$ to $t = $ infinity?

(A) $\displaystyle\int_{0}^{\infty} IR\,dt$

(B) $\displaystyle\int_{0}^{\infty} \varepsilon R\,dt$

(C) $\displaystyle\int_{0}^{\infty} IR^2\,dt$

(D) $\displaystyle\int_{0}^{\infty} I^2 R^2\,dt$

(E) $\displaystyle\int_{0}^{\infty} I^2 R\,dt$

$I = a\,(1 - bt)$

Questions 481–482

A long straight wire carries a current that varies with time according to the equation $I = a(1 - bt)$, where a and b are positive constants. A square conducting loop of side s is placed a distance y above the long wire.

481. When $bt > 1$, the direction of the magnetic field inside the square loop is

(A) out of the page
(B) into the page
(C) toward the top of the page
(D) toward the bottom of the page
(E) toward the left

482. Which of the following expressions could be used to determine the flux through the square loop as a function of time?

(A) Bs^2

(B) $B(y + s)^2$

(C) $\displaystyle\int_{0}^{y+s} \mathbf{B} \cdot d\mathbf{A}$

(D) $\displaystyle\int_{y}^{y+s} \mathbf{B} \cdot d\mathbf{A}$

(E) $\displaystyle\int_{s}^{y+s} \mathbf{B} \cdot d\mathbf{A}$

Questions 483–484

An inductance-resistance (LR) circuit is shown. The switch is closed at time $t = 0$.

483. Which of the following graphs best represents the potential difference V_R across the resistance R as a function of time?

(A) V_R

(B) V_R

(C) V_R

(D) V_R

(E) V_R

484. Which of the following graphs best represents the potential difference V_L across the inductor L as a function of time?

(A)

(B)

(C)

(D)

(E)

485. The ratio L/R has units of

   (A) volts
   (B) amperes
   (C) seconds
   (D) Henrys
   (E) ohms

486. A time-dependent current is described by the equation $I = 3t^2$. The current passes through a 0.5 H inductor. The back emf ε_L across the inductor at a time of 2 s is

(A) −2 V
(B) −3 V
(C) −6 V
(D) −12 V
(E) −24 V

Questions 487–488

The circuit shown includes a battery of emf ε, a switch S, two resistors R, and an inductor L.

487. What is the differential equation that best describes the behavior of the circuit after the switch is connected to a?

(A) $\varepsilon - IR - L\dfrac{dI}{dt} = 0$

(B) $\varepsilon - \dfrac{dI}{dt}R - L\dfrac{d^2I}{dt^2} = 0$

(C) $\varepsilon - \dfrac{dI}{dt}R = 0$

(D) $\varepsilon - L\dfrac{d^2I}{dt^2} = 0$

(E) $\varepsilon - IR - L\dfrac{dI}{dt} = 2R$

488. After a long time, the switch is connected to *b*. What is the differential equation that best describes the behavior of the circuit after the switch is connected to *b*?

(A) $\varepsilon - IR - L\dfrac{dI}{dt} = 0$

(B) $\varepsilon - \dfrac{dI}{dt}R - L\dfrac{d^2I}{dt^2} = 0$

(C) $\varepsilon - 2IR - L\dfrac{dI}{dt} = 0$

(D) $-2IR - L\dfrac{dI}{dt} = 0$

(E) $\varepsilon - \dfrac{dI}{dt}2R - L\dfrac{d^2I}{dt^2} = 0$

489. An ideal circuit consists of a capacitor *C* and inductor *L*. The capacitor is fully charged. The switch is closed at time *t* = 0. Which of the following statements is true of the behavior of the circuit after the switch is closed?

(A) The capacitor will discharge through the inductor, and the current will decrease to zero.

(B) The capacitor will discharge through the inductor, transferring potential energy to kinetic energy.

(C) The capacitor will discharge through the inductor, transferring energy to the inductor, then the inductor will recharge the capacitor.

(D) The capacitor will discharge through the inductor, and the inductor will store the charge.

(E) The capacitor will not discharge through the inductor, so there will be no current.

490. Which of the Maxwell's equations below indicates that there are no magnetic monopoles?

(A) $\int E \cdot dA = \dfrac{q_{enc}}{\varepsilon_o}$

(B) $\int B \cdot dA = 0$

(C) $\int B \cdot dl = \mu_o I_{enc}$

(D) $\varepsilon = \int E \cdot dl = \dfrac{-d\Phi}{dt}$

(E) $\int g \cdot dA = -4\pi GM$

491. Which of the Maxwell's equations below relates electric flux to charge enclosed in a closed surface?

(A) $\int E \cdot dA = \dfrac{q_{enc}}{\varepsilon_o}$

(B) $\int B \cdot dA = 0$

(C) $\int B \cdot dl = \mu_o I_{enc}$

(D) $\varepsilon = \int E \cdot dl = \dfrac{-d\Phi}{dt}$

(E) $\int g \cdot dA = -4\pi GM$

492. Which of the Maxwell's equations below relates current to magnetic field?

(A) $\int E \cdot dA = \dfrac{q_{enc}}{\varepsilon_o}$

(B) $\int B \cdot dA = 0$

(C) $\int B \cdot dl = \mu_o I_{enc}$

(D) $\varepsilon = \int E \cdot dl = \dfrac{-d\Phi}{dt}$

(E) $\int g \cdot dA = -4\pi GM$

493. Which of the Maxwell's equations below relates the electric field produced to a changing magnetic flux?

(A) $\int E \cdot dA = \dfrac{q_{enc}}{\varepsilon_o}$

(B) $\int B \cdot dA = 0$

(C) $\int B \cdot dl = \mu_o I_{enc}$

(D) $\varepsilon = \int E \cdot dl = \dfrac{-d\Phi}{dt}$

(E) $\int g \cdot dA = -4\pi GM$

494. Which of the Maxwell's equations below relates the gravitational field to mass?

(A) $\int E \cdot dA = \dfrac{q_{enc}}{\varepsilon_o}$

(B) $\int B \cdot dA = 0$

(C) $\int B \cdot dl = \mu_o I_{enc}$

(D) $\varepsilon = \int E \cdot dl = \dfrac{-d\Phi}{dt}$

(E) $\int g \cdot dA = -4\pi GM$

Free Response

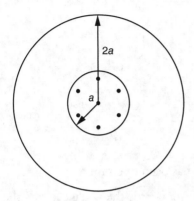

Questions 495–497

A circular region of radius a has a magnetic field B passing through it in an outward direction and perpendicular to the page. A circular conducting loop of radius a is placed in the magnetic field, and a conducting loop of radius $2a$ is placed around the magnetic field. The magnetic field is increasing at a rate dB/dt. Both loops have a resistance R.

495. On the diagram above, indicate the direction of the current I in the smaller loop.

496. In terms of the given quantities, determine the induced current I_1 in the smaller loop.

497. In terms of the given quantities, determine the induced current I_2 in the larger loop.

Questions 498–500

The switch S in the LR circuit shown has been open for a long time.

498. When the switch is connected to a, what is the voltage across the inductor L?

499. After a long time, what is the current through the 2 Ω resistor?

500. After the switch has been connected to a for a long time, what is the energy stored in the inductor?

Chapter 1: Kinematics

1. (C) The time of fall is $t = \sqrt{\dfrac{2y}{g}} = \sqrt{\dfrac{2(80 \text{ m})}{10 \text{ m/s}^2}} = 4$ s.

$$x = v_x t = \left(20\frac{\text{m}}{\text{s}}\right)(4 \text{ s}) = 80 \text{ m}$$

2. (A) The vertical acceleration is constant, so the vertical velocity increases linearly with time.

3. (D) The vertical velocity is $v_y = gt = \left(10\dfrac{\text{m}}{\text{s}^2}\right)(4 \text{ s}) = 40\dfrac{\text{m}}{\text{s}}$.

We use the Pythagorean theorem to relate the horizontal and vertical velocities to the speed:

$$v = \sqrt{v_x^2 + v_y^2} = \sqrt{(20 \text{ m/s})^2 + (40 \text{ m/s})^2} = 44\frac{\text{m}}{\text{s}}$$

4. (B) $= \dfrac{2x_1}{t^2} = \dfrac{2(10 \text{ m})}{(2 \text{ s})^2} = 5 \text{ m/s}^2$. Then $v_1 = at = \left(5\dfrac{\text{m}}{\text{s}^2}\right)(2 \text{ s}) = 10\dfrac{\text{m}}{\text{s}}$

5. (D) The time for 100 m is the sum of the time for the first 10 m and the time for the next 90 m. The time for the sprinter to run 90 m at a constant speed is $t_2 = \dfrac{x_2}{v_1} = \dfrac{90 \text{ m}}{10\dfrac{\text{m}}{\text{s}}} = 9$ s. The total time is $2 \text{ s} + 9 \text{ s} = 11$ s.

6. (C) $a = \dfrac{2y}{t^2} = \dfrac{2(1.2 \text{ m})}{(1.5 \text{ s})^2} = 1.1$ s

7. (A) The package moves upward with the same speed as the helicopter (+3 m/s), rises to its maximum height, then falls back downward. When the package once again reaches the height from which the rope broke, it will be traveling at 3 m/s downward. The speed v_f at which the package strikes the ground is

$$v_f = \sqrt{2ax + v_i^2} = \sqrt{2\left(10\frac{\text{m}}{\text{s}^2}\right)(8 \text{ m}) + \left(3\frac{\text{m}}{\text{s}}\right)^2} = 13\frac{\text{m}}{\text{s}}$$

8. (B) The time of fall is $t = \sqrt{\dfrac{2y}{g}} = \sqrt{\dfrac{2(1.0 \text{ m})}{10 \text{ m/s}^2}} = 0.44$ s.

$$x = v_x t = \left(5\frac{\text{m}}{\text{s}}\right)(0.44 \text{ s}) = 2.3 \text{ m}$$

9. (A) The horizontal range is the same for complementary angles provided the launch speed remains the same. $90° - 60° = 30°$.

10. (B) The cart moves with constant velocity on the level part of the track, then has negative acceleration (negative slope) as it rolls up the hill, then positive acceleration (positive slope) when it rolls down the hill, then continues on the level track with the same velocity as it initially was moving.

11. (C) The speed of the particle is found using the Pythagorean theorem after determining the horizontal and vertical components of the velocity.

$$v_x = v_{ix} + a_x t = 3\frac{\text{m}}{\text{s}} + \left(6\frac{\text{m}}{\text{s}^2}\right)(4 \text{ s}) = 27\frac{\text{m}}{\text{s}}$$

$$v_y = v_{iy} + a_y t = 0 + \left(4\frac{\text{m}}{\text{s}^2}\right)(4 \text{ s}) = 16\frac{\text{m}}{\text{s}}$$

$$v = \sqrt{v_x^2 + v_y^2} = \sqrt{(27 \text{ m/s})^2 + (16 \text{ m/s})^2} = 31\frac{\text{m}}{\text{s}}$$

12. (D) The total displacement is found by applying the Pythagorean theorem after determining the horizontal and vertical components of the displacement.

$$x = x_i + v_{ix}t + \frac{1}{2}a_x t^2 = 0 + \left(3\frac{\text{m}}{\text{s}}\right)(4 \text{ s}) + \frac{1}{2}\left(6\frac{\text{m}}{\text{s}^2}\right)(4 \text{ s})^2 = 60 \text{ m}$$

$$y = y_i + v_{iy}t + \frac{1}{2}a_y t^2 = 0 + 0 + \frac{1}{2}\left(4\frac{\text{m}}{\text{s}^2}\right)(4 \text{ s})^2 = 32 \text{ m}$$

$$r = \sqrt{x^2 + y^2} = \sqrt{(60 \text{ m})^2 + (32 \text{ m})^2} = 68 \text{ m}$$

13. (E) The acceleration (due to gravity) can be found by

$$y = v_{iy}t + \frac{1}{2}gt^2$$

$$g = \frac{2(y - v_{iy}t)}{t^2} = \frac{2\left[2 \text{ m} - \left(6\frac{\text{m}}{\text{s}}\right)(2 \text{ s})\right]}{(2 \text{ s})^2} = 10\frac{\text{m}}{\text{s}^2}$$

14. (B) The graph crosses the time axis at 8 s and 36 s, indicating velocity of zero at these times.

15. (B) The graph crosses the time axis at 8 s and 36 s, indicating velocity of zero at these times, and going from positive velocity to negative velocity, thus turning around and changing direction.

16. (B) The initial horizontal velocity $v_x = v_o$, and the time of fall is $t = \sqrt{\dfrac{2y}{g}} = \sqrt{\dfrac{2D\sin\theta}{g}}$. The vertical velocity at time t is $v_y = gt = g\left(\sqrt{\dfrac{2D\sin\theta}{g}}\right)$. Using the Pythagorean theorem to find the speed of the ball,

$$v_f = \sqrt{v_x^2 + v_y^2}$$

$$v_f = (v_o^2 + 2D\sin\theta g)^{\frac{1}{2}}$$

17. (D) First we calculate the time it takes for the projectile to reach maximum height, where the vertical velocity is zero:

$$v_{iy} = gt$$

$$t_{top} = \frac{v_{iy}}{g} = \frac{40\,\dfrac{m}{s}\sin 60°}{g} = 3.5 \text{ s}$$

The time it takes for the projectile to reach its original height is twice this time: $2ty = 7.0$ s. The time it takes for the projectile to fall the additional 20 m is

$$t = \sqrt{\frac{2y}{g}} = \sqrt{\frac{2(20 \text{ m})}{10 \text{ m/s}^2}} = 2.0 \text{ s. The total time of flight is } 7.0 \text{ s} + 2.0 \text{ s} = 9.0 \text{ s.}$$

18. (E) The speed is found by separating the variables:

$$a = \frac{dv}{dt} = -kv$$

$$-\int kdt = \int_{v_o}^{v} \frac{dv}{v}$$

$$-kt = \ln v]_{v_o}^{v}$$

$$v = v_o e^{-kt}$$

19. (B) The initial velocity of the filters is zero, then they begin falling at the acceleration due to gravity, but the air resistance decreases the acceleration until the velocity is constant. In other words, the slope (acceleration) of the graph decreases as it falls.

20. (D) At maximum height, the vertical velocity is zero. Initially, the vertical velocity $v_y = (8 \text{ m/s})\sin 30° = 4$ m/s. The time to reach the top (when the vertical velocity is zero) is given by $t_{top} = \dfrac{v_{iy}}{g} = \dfrac{4\dfrac{\text{m}}{\text{s}}}{10\dfrac{\text{m}}{\text{s}^2}} = 0.4$ s. The height to the top is

$$y = \frac{1}{2}gt^2 = \frac{1}{2}\left(10\frac{\text{m}}{\text{s}^2}\right)(0.4 \text{ s})^2 = 0.8 \text{ m}$$

21. (E) Since the velocity function is $v = \left(v_o^2 + \dfrac{Ct^2}{m}\right)$, the velocity is never zero, even at $t = 0$.

22. (D) The acceleration is the derivative of the velocity function with respect to time.

$$a = \frac{dv}{dt} = \frac{d}{dt}\left(v_o^2 + \frac{Ct^2}{m}\right) = \left(0 + \frac{2Ct}{m}\right) = \left(\frac{2Ct}{m}\right)$$

23. (E) Since the area under the graph for Car Q is greater than the area under the graph for Car P, at 10 s, Car Q has more displacement than Car P.

24. (A) The area under each graph is the same, indicating the same displacement during the 20 s trip.

25. (C) The area under the graph is 10 m + 20 m + 10 m − 10 m = +30 m. The last 10 m area is negative because it is under the axis.

26. (E) The distance traveled in the first 2 s with no acceleration is

$$x = v_i t = \left(20\frac{\text{m}}{\text{s}}\right)(2 \text{ s}) = 40 \text{ m}$$

The additional distance the car travels while it is slowing down during the next 4 s is

$$x = v_i t + \frac{1}{2}at^2 = \left(20\frac{\text{m}}{\text{s}}\right)(4 \text{ s}) + \frac{1}{2}\left(-4\frac{\text{m}}{\text{s}^2}\right)(4 \text{ s})^2 = 48 \text{ m}$$

The total distance traveled then is 40 m + 48 m = 88 m.

27. (C) The car accelerates positively in the first time interval, then moves with a constant velocity ($a = 0$) during the second time interval, then accelerates negatively during the third time interval, then again has zero acceleration during the fourth time interval. The position vs. time graph would curve upward, then constant slope, then curve downward, and the velocity vs. time graph would have a constant slope, zero slope, then a constant negative slope to show this motion.

28. (C) Since the plane's engines can make it move up to 200 km/h, without wind it could travel 100 km in a half hour. Since the crosswind would add distance to the flight, it would take more than a half hour for the plane to travel 100 km.

29. (E) The acceleration of the object would have to remove the x-component of the velocity and add a vertically upward component, the acceleration would have to be directed up and to the left to cancel the horizontal motion and add an upward vertical motion.

30. (C) The velocity is the time integral of acceleration, and the position is the integral of velocity.

$$v = \int adt = \int 4t^2 dt = \frac{4}{3}t^3$$

$$x = \int vdt = \int \frac{4}{3}t^3 dt = \frac{1}{3}t^4$$

At $t = 3$ s, $\frac{1}{3}(3 \text{ s})^4 = 27$ m

31. (B) The time of flight for the ball and the rock is the same: $t = \sqrt{\frac{2y}{g}} = \sqrt{\frac{2(80 \text{ m})}{10 \text{ m/s}^2}} = 4$ s. The horizontal distance the projected rock travels is 40 m. The horizontal speed is $v_x = \frac{x}{t} = \frac{40 \text{ m}}{4 \text{ s}} = 10\frac{\text{m}}{\text{s}}$.

32. (C) Acceleration is the derivative of velocity with respect to time, so the derivative of the velocity with respect to time is 3.8 m/s².

33. (D) The kinematic equation for acceleration gives $a = \frac{v_f - v_i}{t} = \frac{24\frac{\text{m}}{\text{s}} - 0}{4 \text{ s}} = 6\frac{\text{m}}{\text{s}^2}$.
The distance traveled is

$$x = x_i + v_i t + \frac{1}{2}at^2 = 0 + 0 + \frac{1}{2}\left(6\frac{\text{m}}{\text{s}^2}\right)(4 \text{ s})^2 = 48 \text{ m}$$

34. (E) When the ball is dropped, it has a vertical velocity (free fall) and a horizontal velocity equal to the velocity of the train. It will follow a parabolic path as it falls, and the total speed can be found by combining the horizontal and vertical velocities using the Pythagorean theorem.

35. (B) At the top of its flight, the velocity of the ball is zero, since it's turning around to come back down. Gravity continually causes the acceleration, so the ball's acceleration is g everywhere during its flight.

36. (B) Let the initial velocity of the dart be v. Then the vertical component of the initial velocity is $v \sin \theta = v \sin 45 = \dfrac{\sqrt{2}}{2} v$. Since the general equation relating the maximum height of the dart is $v = \sqrt{2gh}$, then $\dfrac{\sqrt{2}}{2} v = \sqrt{2gh}$, giving a height of $2h$ for the initial speed v. So the new height is 2 m.

37. (C) The velocity at point A is horizontal and constant, and equal to the initial horizontal velocity of the projectile.

38. (E) The acceleration everywhere on the flight path is g, which is always directed downward.

39. (A) In the first time interval, the position vs. time graph curves upward, indicating a positive acceleration, depicted on the velocity vs. time graph as a line with a constant positive slope. The constant slope in the second interval indicates a constant velocity, producing a horizontal line on the velocity vs. time graph. Then the position vs. time graph shows the object slowing down with a negative acceleration, indicated by a line with a negative slope on the velocity vs. time graph, and zero velocity in the last interval.

40. (B) The acceleration is the derivative of the velocity with respect to time:

$$a = \frac{dv}{dt} = \frac{d}{dt}\left(16t - \frac{1}{2}t^4\right) = 16 - 2t^3$$

41. (C) At terminal velocity, acceleration is zero. We set the equation for acceleration equal to zero, solve for time, then substitute that time back into the equation for velocity:

$a = 0 = 16 - 2t^3$ giving $t = 2$ s. Then substituting $t = 2$ s into $v = 16t - \frac{1}{2}\,t^4$ gives $v = 24$ m/s.

42. (B) Since the horizontal distance x is proportional to horizontal velocity v_x for the same amount of time of fall (same vertical height), the student would have to jump twice as fast to land twice as far away.

43. (D) The distance an object falls can be found by $y = \dfrac{1}{2}gt^2$. Rearranging for g, we get

$$g = \frac{2y}{t^2} = \frac{2(2\ \mathrm{m})}{(1\ \mathrm{s})^2} = 4\frac{\mathrm{m}}{\mathrm{s}^2}$$

44. (A) The average speed of the car is equal to the total distance divided by the total time:

$$v_{avg} = \frac{\Delta x}{\Delta t} = \frac{500\ \mathrm{m}}{90\ \mathrm{s}} = 5.6\frac{\mathrm{m}}{\mathrm{s}}$$

45. (C) The object accelerates at a constant rate, positively in the first interval, then negatively in the second interval. The net result is that whatever speed it gained in the first interval, it lost in the second interval. The displacement is not zero, since the object continued gaining velocity throughout the trip.

46. $v = at = \left(5\dfrac{\mathrm{m}}{\mathrm{s}^2}\right)(5\ \mathrm{s}) = 25\dfrac{\mathrm{m}}{\mathrm{s}}$

47. $x = \dfrac{1}{2}at^2 = \dfrac{1}{2}\left(5\dfrac{\mathrm{m}}{\mathrm{s}^2}\right)(5\ \mathrm{s})^2 = 63\ \mathrm{m}$

48. From 0 to 5 s, the elevator is accelerating upward with a constant acceleration of 5 m/s², so the v vs. t graph is linear, then when the acceleration is zero from 5 s to 10 s, the velocity is constant at 25 m/s. From 10 s to 15 s, the acceleration is negative and constant, producing a linear velocity with a negative slope. Since the positive acceleration matches the negative acceleration throughout from 0 to 15 s, the object is at rest from 15s to 20 s.

49. Since the horizontal velocity is $v_x = 6$ m/s, then the horizontal displacement is $x = v_x t = 6t$. Then

$$v_y = \frac{dy}{dt} = \frac{d}{dt}[2(6t)^2] = 72t$$

50. The horizontal acceleration is zero (constant velocity), so the only acceleration is vertically upward. Imagine a projectile following a parabolic path, in which the acceleration due to gravity is vertical.

Chapter 2: Dynamics: Newton's Laws of Motion

51. (D) A ball moving in a circle has a centripetal force acting on it. A space probe does not need a net force to travel at a constant velocity, but will continue due to its inertia. An object changing any component of its velocity is accelerating, so there must be a net force acting on it.

52. (C) Newton's 3rd law states that the objects apply equal and opposite forces to each other, although the resulting accelerations will not be the same for each.

53. (A) The law of inertia states that the object must be moving with a constant velocity, and Graph (A) indicates constant velocity.

54. (B) According to Newton's 2nd law, the acceleration of the blocks is the net force divided by the total mass of the blocks:

$$a = \frac{F_{net}}{m} = \frac{18 \text{ N}}{6 \text{ kg}} = 3 \frac{\text{m}}{\text{s}^2}$$

55. (B) The tension in the cord only has to accelerate the 2 kg mass at 3 m/s².

$$T = ma = (2 \text{ kg})\left(3\frac{\text{m}}{\text{s}^2}\right) = 6 \text{ N}$$

56. (D) Since the pulley has no mass, the net force accelerating the system of blocks is the weight of the 2 kg block, which is 20 N. The combined mass of the system that is being accelerated is 3 kg, so the acceleration of the system is

$$a = \frac{F_{net}}{m} = \frac{20 \text{ N}}{3 \text{ kg}} = 6.7 \frac{\text{m}}{\text{s}^2} \text{ or } \frac{2}{3}g$$

57. **(A)** Since the initial velocity of the 2 kg block is zero, the speed after descending a distance D can be found by

$$v = \sqrt{2aD} = \sqrt{2\left(\frac{2}{3}g\right)D} = \sqrt{\frac{4D}{3}}$$

58. **(B)** The horizontal component of tension in the slanted cord must equal the tension in the horizontal cord, so the tension in the slanted cord must be greater than the tension in the horizontal cord.

59. **(C)** The horizontal component of tension in the slanted cord T_v must equal the tension in the horizontal cord. The tension in the horizontal cord = $T_v \cos 60° = \frac{1}{2} T_v$.

60. **(A)** The initial velocity is c when time $t = 0$.

61. **(B)** The net force is given by Newton's 2nd law:

$$F_{net} = ma = m\frac{dv}{dt} = m(3bt^2) = 3mbT^2$$

62. **(B)** For an object moving with constant acceleration, the distance traveled along the plane is proportional to the square of the time. Equivalently, the distance between each second increases with the odd integers: 1, 3, 5, 7. . . . So if the block travels 1 m in the first second, it will travel 3 m in the next second.

63. **(C)** Since the particle is following a parabolic path (imagine a projectile moving under the influence of gravity), the horizontal velocity is constant, and the only acceleration is vertical. Since the particle's path is curving upward, there must be a vertical force and acceleration.

64. **(E)** According to Newton's 2nd law, the acceleration of the blocks is the net force divided by the total mass of the blocks:

$$a = \frac{F_{net}}{m} = \frac{24\ N}{6\ kg} = 4\frac{m}{s^2}$$

65. **(B)** The force between the 2 kg block and the 1 kg block only has to accelerate the 1 kg mass at 4 m/s².

$$F = ma = (1\ kg)\left(4\frac{m}{s^2}\right) = 4\ N$$

66. (D) The force acting on the puck removes the horizontal motion of the puck and adds an acceleration in the vertical direction, so the force must be directed upward and to the left.

67. (E) Since the block is sliding at a constant velocity, the frictional force directed up the incline must equal the component of the weight along the incline, $f = mg\sin\theta$. The coefficient of friction is $\mu = \dfrac{f}{N}$, where N is the normal force and is equal and opposite to the component of the weight that points downward and perpendicular to the plane, that is $N = mg\cos\theta$. Substituting into our equation for the coefficient of friction,

$$\mu = \frac{f}{N} = \frac{mg\sin\theta}{mg\cos\theta} = \tan\theta = \tan30° = 0.6$$

68. (B) The net force is zero when the acceleration is zero.

$$v_y = \frac{dy}{dt} = \frac{d}{dt}[8t - 4t^2 + t^3] = 8 - 8t + 3t^2$$

$$a_y = \frac{dv_y}{dt} = \frac{d}{dt}[8 - 8t + 3t^2] = -8 + 6t$$

The acceleration and net force are zero when $t = 4/3$ s.

69. (E) The gravitational force is constant near the surface of the Earth, and the air resistance decreases as the ball rises, since the ball's velocity is decreasing.

70. (C) The weight of the 800 kg elevator is 8000 N. The net force acting on the elevator as it rises is 10000 N − 8000 N = 2000 N upward. The acceleration of the elevator is

$$a = \frac{F_{net}}{m} = \frac{2000 \text{ N}}{800 \text{ kg}} = 2.5 \frac{\text{m}}{\text{s}^2}$$

71. (B) The net force acting on the elevator is still 2000 N, which produces a downward acceleration of 2.5 m/s². The final velocity is zero, which gives an initial velocity of

$$v_i = \sqrt{2ah} = \sqrt{2\left(10\frac{\text{m}}{\text{s}^2}\right)(10 \text{ m})} = 7\frac{\text{m}}{\text{s}}$$

72. (D) The vertical component of F_A must be greater than the vertical component of FB, since it must support more of the weight W due to F_A's larger angle to the horizontal.

73. (C) Since the block is sliding up the plane, the frictional force is directed down the plane. The weight is downward, and the normal force is perpendicular to the surface of the ramp.

74. (A) The frictional force f is directed down the plane along with the component of the weight down the plane, $mg\sin\theta$. The normal force is $N = mg\cos\theta$. The net force is

$$F_{net} = f + mg\sin\theta = ma$$

$$f = (1 \text{ kg})\left(6 \frac{m}{s^2}\right) - (1 \text{ kg})\left(10 \frac{m}{s^2}\right)\sin 30° = 1 \text{ N}$$

75. (B) Since the force is the same in both situations, $m_1a_1 = m_2a_2$. So $(8 \text{ kg})(3 \text{ m/s}^2) = (12 \text{ kg}) a_2$, giving $a_2 = 2 \text{ m/s}^2$.

76. (C) Both blocks accelerate at the same acceleration, but the string only has to accelerate the 2 kg block, which represents 1/3 of the total mass. So the tension in the string only has to apply 1/3 F to accelerate the small block.

77. (B) The upward vertical component of the force is $F\sin\theta$, and this component of the force lightens the normal force, producing a normal force of $mg - F\sin\theta$. The frictional force is then

$$f = \mu N = \mu(mg - F\sin\theta)$$

78. (E) The three tensions T in the ropes must each support 1/3 of the 60-N weight of the block, or $3T = W$.

79. (E) $a = \dfrac{F_{net}}{m} = \dfrac{cv}{m}$

80. (A) The net force accelerating the system is the weight of block m, which is mg. The weight of block m accelerates masses totaling $5m$. So

$$a = \frac{F_{net}}{m} = \frac{mg}{5m} = \frac{1}{5}g$$

81. (B) The net force is now $mg - \frac{1}{2}\, mg = \frac{1}{2}\, mg$. The acceleration is

$$a = \frac{F_{net}}{m} = \frac{\frac{1}{2}\, mg}{5m} = \frac{1}{10}\, g$$

82. (C) The acceleration is produced by the component of the weight that is directed down the incline, $mg\sin\theta$.

$$F_{net} = mg\sin\theta = ma$$

$$a = g\sin\theta = g\left(\frac{3}{5}\right) = 6\ \frac{m}{s^2}$$

83. (D) The normal force is equal and opposite to the component of the weight that is perpendicular to the plane, $N = mg\cos\theta = (10\ N)(4/5) = 8\ N$.

84. (E) The net force acting on the projectile is the weight of the projectile, which is always directed downward.

85. (A) For the ring to be in equilibrium, the vector sum of the forces acting on it must be zero.

86. (C) The acceleration is the derivative of velocity with respect to time, and velocity is the derivative of position with respect to time.

$$v_x = \frac{dx}{dt} = \frac{d}{dt}[2t^2 - 3t^3] = 4t - 9t^2$$

$$a_x = \frac{dv_x}{dt} = \frac{d}{dt}[4t - 9t^2] = 4 - 18t$$

At $t = 1$ s, $F_{net} = ma = m(4 - 18t) = -14\ N$

87. (B) The force becomes negative after $4 - 18t = 0$, when $t = 0.22$ s.

88. (A) The acceleration is the derivative of the velocity with respect to time:

$$a = \frac{dv}{dt} = \frac{d}{dt}[4t^2\ \mathbf{i} + 6t^4\ \mathbf{j}] = 8t\ \mathbf{i} + 24t^3\mathbf{j}$$

89. (E) Newton's 2nd law states that

$$F_{net} = ma = (0.5 \text{ kg})(8t \text{ } \mathbf{i} + 24t^3 \mathbf{j})$$

$$F_x = (0.5 \text{ kg})[8(2 \text{ s})] = 8 \text{ N}$$

$$F_y = (0.5 \text{ kg})[24(2 \text{ s})^3] = 96 \text{ N}$$

$$F_{net} = \sqrt{F_x^2 + F_y^2} = \sqrt{(8 \text{ N})^2 + (96 \text{ N})^2} = 104 \text{ N}$$

90. (D) If the net force is directed perpendicular to the velocity (such as on an object in circular motion), then the force cannot change the speed of the object, only the direction of its velocity.

91. (D) The filter begins from rest ($v = 0$) and begins with a high acceleration, indicated by the high slope at the beginning of the fall. As the filter accelerates, its acceleration decreases due to the increasing resistive force of the air. Eventually, the speed of the filter is constant (terminal velocity).

92. (E) The maximum frictional force that can act on the 2 kg block is

$$f = \mu mg = (0.2)(2 \text{ kg})\left(10 \text{ } \frac{\text{m}}{\text{s}^2} \right) = 4 \text{ N}$$

This frictional force corresponds to a maximum acceleration of the 2 kg block (so that it does not slip off):

$$a = \frac{F_{net}}{m} = \frac{4 \text{ N}}{2 \text{ kg}} = 2 \frac{\text{m}}{\text{s}^2}$$

So the force acting on the 4 kg block cannot accelerate the system (6 kg) by more than 2 m/s².

$$F_{net} = ma = (6 \text{ kg})\left(2 \frac{\text{m}}{\text{s}^2} \right) = 12 \text{ N}$$

93. (B) The maximum acceleration the frictional force can tolerate is 2 m/s². If the 4 kg block is accelerating at 3 m/s², the 2 kg block will appear to accelerate to the left at 1 m/s² *relative to the 4 kg block*. We could also say that the 2 kg block is accelerating at 2 m/s² to the right relative to the table top.

94. The normal force the table exerts on the system is equal to the weight of the system: $2mg + 2mg + 4mg = 8mg$.

95. The net force that accelerates the system is $3mg$. The acceleration of the system then is

$$a = \frac{F_{net}}{m} = \frac{3mg}{5m} = \frac{3}{5}g$$

96. The acceleration of the system is $3/5$ g. The tension in the string is accelerating a total mass of $4m$. The tension in the string is

$$T = ma = 4m\left(\frac{3}{5}g\right) = \frac{12}{5}mg$$

97. Less than $8mg$. While the system is accelerating, the tension in the strings must be less than the corresponding weights. Thus, the effect is that the tensions decrease the normal force acting on the stand as the system accelerates when compared with the system at rest, in which the normal force is simply the sum of the weights.

98. The tension in the string must be 10 N, since it supports the hanging 10 N weight in equilibrium.

99. Since the tension in the string is 10 N, the sum of the frictional force and component of the weight that is perpendicular to the plane ($mg\sin\theta$) must equal 10 N.

$$f + mg\sin\theta = 10 \text{ N}$$

$$f = 10 \text{ N} - (10 \text{ N})\sin37° = 4 \text{ N}$$

100. The net force acting on the block on the incline is $mg\sin\theta - f$. The acceleration of the block on the incline is

$$a = \frac{mg\sin\theta - f}{m} = \frac{(10 \text{ N})\sin37° - 4 \text{ N}}{1 \text{ kg}} = 2\frac{\text{m}}{\text{s}^2}$$

The velocity at the bottom of the incline is

$$v = \sqrt{2aD} = \sqrt{2\left(2\frac{\text{m}}{\text{s}^2}\right)(5 \text{ m})} = 4.5\frac{\text{m}}{\text{s}}$$

Chapter 3: Work, Energy, Power, and Conservation of Energy

101. (C) The work done from 0 to 4 m is equal to the area under the graph, $4\,J + 2\,J = 6\,J$.

102. (C) The change in kinetic energy from 0 to 5 s is equal to the work done during this time. The area under the graph from 0 to 4 m is 6 J, and the area from 4 m to 5 m is $-\frac{1}{2}$ J, giving a change of kinetic energy of $6\,J - \frac{1}{2}\,J = 5.5\,J$.

103. (A) Power is work divided by time: $P = \dfrac{Work}{t} = \dfrac{(Weight)D}{t}$.

104. (D) The general equation for potential energy is $U = mgh$. Both masses have a potential energy, but one is rising and one is descending. So the change in potential energy of the system is

$$m_A gD - m_B gD = (m_A - m_B)gD$$

105. (A) According to the law of conservation of energy, the change in potential energy equals the change in kinetic energy:

$$\frac{1}{2}(m_A + m_B)v^2 = (m_A - m_B)gD$$

Solving for the speed v,

$$v = \sqrt{\frac{(m_A - m_B)}{(m_A + m_B)}gD}$$

106. (E) The work done on the object is equal to the change in kinetic energy of the object. The work done can be estimated by the area under each graph. The least area under the graph corresponds to the least change in kinetic energy.

107. (C) The kinetic energy of the particle is given by $K = \dfrac{1}{2}mv^2$, where v is found by the derivative of position x with respect to time:

$$v = \frac{dx}{dt} = \frac{d}{dt}\left[2t^{\frac{5}{2}}\right] = 5t^{\frac{3}{2}}$$

Then the kinetic energy is

$$K = \frac{1}{2}mv^2 = \frac{1}{2}m\left(5t^{\frac{3}{2}}\right)^2 = \frac{5}{2}mt^3$$

108. (C) Conservation of energy states that the total energy remains constant.

$$U_o + K_o = U_f + K_f + E_{\text{friction}}$$

$$mgh + \frac{1}{2}mv_o^2 = 0 + \frac{1}{2}mv_f^2 + E_{\text{friction}}$$

$$E_{\text{friction}} = mgh + \frac{1}{2}mv_o^2 - \frac{1}{2}mv_f^2$$

$$= (1 \text{ kg})\left(10\frac{m}{s^2}\right)(50 \text{ m}) + \frac{1}{2}(1 \text{ kg})\left(4\frac{m}{s}\right)^2 - \frac{1}{2}(1 \text{ kg})\left(20\frac{m}{s}\right)^2$$

$$E_{\text{friction}} = 308 \text{ J}$$

109. (C) At point P, there is only horizontal velocity $v_x = v\cos 37° = (20 \text{ m/s})$ $\cos 37° = 16$ m/s. So the kinetic energy at point P is

$$K = \frac{1}{2}mv_x^2 = \frac{1}{2}(2 \text{ kg})\left(16\frac{m}{s}\right)^2 = 256 \text{ J}$$

110. (D) By symmetry, the speed at point Q is the same as it was at the beginning of the path.

$$K_Q = \frac{1}{2}mv_Q^2 = \frac{1}{2}(2 \text{ kg})\left(20\frac{m}{s}\right)^2 = 400 \text{ J}$$

111. (D) The height h of the pendulum from which it starts above the lowest point of the swing is

$$h = L - L\cos 30°$$

By conservation of energy,

$$mgh = mg(L - L\cos 30) = \frac{1}{2}mv^2$$

$$v = \sqrt{2g(L - L\cos 30°)}$$

112. (D) The change in kinetic energy corresponds to the net work done on the weight, 15 N − 10 N = 5 N upward. If the question had asked for the work done against gravity only, you would use only the 10 N force.

113. (C) At $x = 0$, $U = 4(0) − 2(0) + 3 = 3$ J.

114. (C) The force is equal to the negative derivative of U with respect to time:

$$F = -\frac{dU}{dx} = -\frac{d}{dx}[4x^2 - 2x + 3] = -8x - 2 = -8\left(\frac{1}{4}\text{ m}\right) - 2 = -4 \text{ N, or a magnitude}$$

of 4 N.

115. (B) The mass of the ball is $m = \dfrac{U}{gh} = \dfrac{30 \text{ J}}{\left(10\dfrac{\text{m}}{\text{s}^2}\right)(5 \text{ m})} = 0.6 \text{ kg}$. Conservation of

energy gives

$$mgh + \frac{1}{2}mv^2 = mgh_{\max}$$

$$h_{\max} = \frac{mgh + \dfrac{1}{2}mv^2}{mg} = \frac{(0.6 \text{ kg})\left(10\dfrac{\text{m}}{\text{s}^2}\right)(5 \text{ m}) + 20 \text{ J}}{(0.6 \text{ kg})\left(10\dfrac{\text{m}}{\text{s}^2}\right)} = 8.3 \text{ m}$$

116. (A) $F = \dfrac{P}{v} = \dfrac{6 \text{ W}}{3\dfrac{\text{m}}{\text{s}}} = 2 \text{ N}$

117. (D) The work done by the weightlifter against gravity is

$$W = mgh = (100 \text{ kg})\left(10\frac{\text{m}}{\text{s}^2}\right)(2 \text{ m}) = 2000 \text{ J}$$

118. (C) The power developed by the weightlifter is

$$P = \frac{W}{t} = \frac{2000 \text{ J}}{2 \text{ s}} = 1000 \text{ W}$$

119. (B) The force is given by the negative of the derivative (slope) of the U vs. x graph, which is constant between $x = 3$ and $x = 4$.

120. (C) The maximum energy of the particle is 3 J, and it would only take 2 J for the particle to reach $x = 1$.

121. (B) The potential energy function is equal to the negative integral of the force over the position x:

$$U(x) = -\int F(x)dx$$

$$= -\int\left(-3x^2 - 2x - 4\right)dx = x^3 + x^2 + 4x = 2^3 + 2^2 + 4(2) = 20 \text{ J}$$

122. (E) $F = -dU/dx = -4x - 1$, so the force is linearly related to the position x, with a negative slope.

123. (A) The net work done depends on the change in potential energy Δmgh, which depends on the mass of the object and the height between P and Q.

124. (A) Only the horizontal component of the force gives the block a horizontal displacement and thus does work on the block. The horizontal component of the force is $F\sin\theta$, and it is applied through a horizontal distance x. So, $W = Fx\sin\theta$.

125. (D) Since the block is moving with a constant speed, the frictional force must be equal to the horizontal component of the applied force. The coefficient of friction is equal to the frictional force divided by the normal force. The normal force is the sum of the vertical component of the applied force and the weight of the block.

$$\mu = \frac{f}{N} = \frac{F\sin\theta}{F\cos\theta + mg}$$

126. (A) Since the centripetal force acting on the electron is always perpendicular to the velocity of the electron, the force can do no net work when the electron returns to its starting position (1 revolution).

127. (B) Between x_o and $3x_o$, the potential energy of the particle decreases by $2U_o$, which must have been converted to kinetic energy.

128. (D) At the position $3x_o$, the potential energy is U_o. Since the total energy is $3U_o$, the kinetic energy K is equal to $2U_o$.

$$K = \frac{1}{2}mv^2 = 2U_o, \text{ giving } v = \sqrt{\frac{2U_o}{m}}.$$

129. (C) Conservation of energy states that the total energy of the pendulum is equal to the sum of the potential energy and kinetic energy. If the total energy is 20 J and the potential energy is 10 J, the remaining 10 J of energy is kinetic energy.

130. (C) If gravity does +100 J in moving the block downward from a height h, it must do −100 J of work as it slides back up to a height h, since gravity is a conservative force.

131. (D) The time of fall is $t = \sqrt{\dfrac{2y}{g}} = \sqrt{\dfrac{2(45 \text{ m})}{10 \text{ m/s}^2}} = 3$ s. The initial horizontal velocity is

$$v_x = \frac{x}{t} = \frac{60 \text{ m}}{3 \text{ s}} = 20 \frac{\text{m}}{\text{s}}$$

132. (A) Using conservation of energy,

$$mgh + \frac{1}{2}mv_x^2 = \frac{1}{2}mv^2$$

$$(5 \text{ kg})\left(10\frac{\text{m}}{\text{s}^2}\right)(45 \text{ m}) + \frac{1}{2}(5 \text{ kg})\left(20\frac{\text{m}}{\text{s}}\right)^2 = \frac{1}{2}(5 \text{ kg})v^2$$

$$v = 12 \text{ m/s}$$

133. (B) The kinetic energy is high at the beginning, then decreases to zero at the top of the path of the ball, then increases as the ball falls.

134. (B) The potential energy graph would be the inverse of the kinetic energy graph, starting low near the ground at the beginning of the flight, increasing with height as it rises, then decreasing as it falls back to the ground.

135. (D) The drop in height of the block is $h = R - R\cos\theta$. The kinetic energy at θ is equal to the drop in potential energy:

$$K = mg(R - R\cos\theta)$$

136. (D) The speed of the block at θ can be found by setting the equation for kinetic energy equal to the equation for potential energy:

$$K = \frac{1}{2}mv^2 = mg(R - R\cos\theta), \text{ giving } v = \sqrt{2g(R - R\cos\theta)}$$

137. (D) At a point halfway down the ramp, $\theta = 45°$. Using conservation of energy (from the top),

$$h = R\sin45°$$

$$mgh = mgR\sin45° = \frac{1}{2}mv^2$$

$$v = \sqrt{2gR\sin45°}$$

138. (D) The energy expended by the machine is

$$E = \int_0^{10} Pdt = \int_0^{10}(4t^3 + 3t^2 - 2)dt = [t^4 + t^3 - 2t]_0^{10} = 10,080 \text{ J}$$

139. (B) A kilowatt-hour has units of power × time, which is energy.

140. (C) Since the crate is moving at a constant speed, the applied force must be equal and opposite to the frictional force.

$$F = f = \mu mg$$

The rate at which work is done is power:

$$P = fv = \mu mgv$$

141. (D) The height above the bottom of the swing is $h = L - L\cos\theta$. The potential energy at this height is

$$mgh = mg(L - L\cos\theta)$$

This potential energy is converted to kinetic energy according to conservation of energy:

$$mgh = mg(L - L\cos\theta) = \frac{1}{2}mv^2$$

The speed v at the bottom of the swing is $\sqrt{2g(L - L\cos\theta)}$.

142. (A) The potential energy at the top of the ramp is mgr. All of this potential energy is dissipated by friction when it comes to rest at the end of the surface.

143. (B) The kinetic energy just after it strikes the floor is equal to the potential energy at the height of 4 m.

$$mgh = \frac{1}{2}mv^2$$

$$v = \sqrt{2gh} = \sqrt{2\left(10\frac{m}{s^2}\right)(4 \text{ m})} = 9\frac{m}{s}$$

144. (B) If there were no energy lost, the ball would rebound at 12 m/s and rise to a height h after the bounce:

$$mgh = \frac{1}{2}mv^2$$

$$h = \frac{v^2}{2g} = \frac{\left(12\frac{m}{s}\right)^2}{2\left(10\frac{m}{s^2}\right)} = 7.2 \text{ m}$$

The potential energy associated with this height is

$$mgh = (1 \text{ kg})\left(10\frac{\text{m}}{\text{s}^2}\right)(7.2 \text{ m}) = 72 \text{ J}$$

But the ball only rises to 4 m,

$$mgh = (1 \text{ kg})\left(10\frac{\text{m}}{\text{s}^2}\right)(4 \text{ m}) = 40 \text{ J}$$

The fraction of energy lost is

$$\frac{72 \text{ J} - 40 \text{ J}}{72 \text{ J}} = 0.44$$

145. The force the girl has to apply to keep the box moving at a constant velocity must be equal and opposite to the frictional force:

$$F = f = \mu N = \mu mg = (0.4)(20 \text{ kg})\left(10\frac{\text{m}}{\text{s}^2}\right) = 80 \text{ N}$$

146. Work = the product of force and distance: $W = Fd = (80 \text{ N})(6 \text{ m}) = 480 \text{ J}$

147. Power is the rate at which work is done and is equal to the product of force and speed:

$$P = Fv = (80 \text{ N})\left(2\frac{\text{m}}{\text{s}}\right) = 160 \text{ watts}$$

148. The potential energy, as well as total energy, is maximum at $x = 2$ m.

149. When the displacement is −1 m, the potential energy is 0.5 J. Since the total energy is 3.0 J, the kinetic energy must be 2.5 J.

150. The kinetic energy is 3.0 J, since the potential energy is zero at $x = 0$. So,

$$K = \frac{1}{2}mv^2 = 3.0 \text{ J}$$

$$\frac{1}{2}(2 \text{ kg})v^2 = 3.0 \text{ J}$$

$$v = \sqrt{3} \text{ m/s}$$

Chapter 4: Impulse, Linear Momentum, and Conservation of Linear Momentum

151. (A) For this inelastic collision, conservation of momentum states that

$$m_1 v_1 + m_2 v_2 = (m_1 + m_2) v'$$

$$v' = \frac{m_1 v_1 + m_2 v_2}{(m_1 + m_2)} = \frac{-(3 \text{ kg})\left(2\dfrac{\text{m}}{\text{s}}\right) + (4 \text{ kg})\left(1\dfrac{\text{m}}{\text{s}}\right)}{(3 \text{ kg} + 4 \text{ kg})} = \frac{2}{7}\dfrac{\text{m}}{\text{s}}$$

Since the 3.0 kg object has more initial momentum (to the left) than the 4.0 kg object (to the right), the resulting momentum after the collision is to the left.

152. (C) By definition, a perfectly elastic collision conserves both momentum and kinetic energy.

153. (D) The area under the graph represents the impulse acting on the mass. The area under the graph from 0 s to 2 s is 4 N s, the impulse from 2 s to 4 s is 8 N s, and the impulse from 4 s to 6 s is 4 N s. The total impulse is 16 N s.

154. (C) The impulse is equal to the change in momentum of the mass:

$$16 \text{ N s} = m(v_f - v_i) = 2 \text{ kg}(v_f - 0)$$

$$v_f = 8\dfrac{\text{m}}{\text{s}}$$

155. (D) The horizontal component of the momentum of the ball when it strikes the wall is $mv\cos\theta$. The horizontal component of the momentum of the ball after the collision is $-mv\cos\theta$, giving a change of momentum of $-mv\cos\theta - (-mv\cos\theta) = 2mv\cos\theta$.

156. (A) Because the blocks have different masses, their respective accelerations will be different, but the impulse applied to each mass and the product of each mass and its corresponding velocity (momentum) will be the same.

157. (C) The mass of the car is m_c, and the mass of the sand is m_s. Momentum is conserved as sand is added to the car:

$$m_c v_c = (m_c + m_s) v'$$

$$(1000 \text{ kg})\left(3\dfrac{\text{m}}{\text{s}}\right) = (1000 \text{ kg} + m_s)\left(1\dfrac{\text{m}}{\text{s}}\right)$$

$$m_s = 2000 \text{ kg}$$

158. (E) The momentum in the y-direction before the collision is zero, so the y-component of the momentum after the collision must be zero as well. The vertical component of the momentum of the 0.4 kg ball is downward, so the vertical component of the momentum of the 0.2 kg ball must be upward.

$$m_1 v_1 = -m_2 v_2$$

$$(0.4 \text{ kg})\left(2\frac{m}{s}\right) = (0.2 \text{ kg})v_2$$

$$v_2 = 4\frac{m}{s} \text{ upward}$$

159. (C) The total momentum in both the x- and y-directions is the same both before and after the collision, zero in the x-direction and −16 kg m/s in the y-direction.

160. (B) The vertical component of the velocity of the 2 kg ball after the collision is $v_y = \dfrac{p_y}{m} = \dfrac{16\frac{\text{kgm}}{s}}{2 \text{ kg}} = 8\frac{m}{s}$, and the horizontal component of the velocity of the 2 kg ball after the collision is $v_x = \dfrac{p_x}{m} = \dfrac{9\frac{\text{kgm}}{s}}{2 \text{ kg}} = 4.5\frac{m}{s}$. The speed of the 2 kg ball is then

$$v = \sqrt{v_x^2 + v_y^2} = \sqrt{\left(8\frac{m}{s}\right)^2 + \left(4.5\frac{m}{s}\right)^2} = 9.2\frac{m}{s}$$

161. (B) The impulse J imparted to the ball is equal to the change in momentum of the ball.

$$\Delta p = m\Delta v = (0.3 \text{ kg})\left(20\frac{m}{s}\right) = 6 \text{ N s}$$

162. (B) When the skaters push away from each other, they apply equal and opposite impulses to each other, and thus their change in momenta are equal.

163. (C) The x- and y-components of the momentum of $2m$ are equal and opposite to the x- and y-components of the momenta of the other two masses. So, the momentum of mass $2m$ after the explosion is

$$2mv' = \sqrt{(mv)^2 + (mv)^2}, \text{ giving } v' = \frac{\sqrt{2}}{2}v$$

164. (D) The momentum vector of mass $2m$ must be equal and opposite to the resultant momentum of the two smaller masses. The resultant momentum of the two smaller masses is down and to the left, so the resultant momentum of $2m$ must be up and to the right.

165. (C) The momentum of the center of mass of the system is equal to the vector sum of the individual momenta of the blocks:

$$-2mv + mv = 3mv_{CM}$$

$$v_{CM} = \frac{1}{3}(2 \text{ kg} + 1 \text{ kg})v$$

166. (A) The center of mass will continue as if the object had not exploded, so its velocity will be horizontally directed to the right.

167. (A) The center of mass will continue as if the object had not exploded, so it will continue on the parabolic path and land at the place where the object would have landed had it not exploded.

168. (B) The pieces of clay have equal and opposite x-components of momentum so they will cancel each other out, leaving only vertically downward momentum after the collision.

169. (B) The horizontal components of the momenta before the collision are equal and opposite, so there is only vertical momentum after the collision.

$$2mv_o \sin 30° = 2mv'$$

$$v' = \frac{1}{2}v_o$$

170. (A) By conservation of momentum,

$$mv = (m + 2m)v_{CM}$$

$$v_{CM} = \left(\frac{m}{m + 2m}\right)v$$

171. (C) Since the two masses are equal and collide elastically, the first mass stops and the second mass takes all of its momentum, moving at 3 m/s.

172. (B) The second and third masses collide and stick together, doubling the mass and halving the speed, so ½ (3 m/s) = 1.5 m/s.

173. (D) Since there is no x-component of momentum before the collision, the momentum of ball 1 must have a positive x-component of momentum after the collision as well as a positive y-component of momentum to be added to the y-component of momentum of ball 2. So the momentum of ball 1 must point upward and to the right.

174. (E) The product $F\Delta t$ is impulse and is equal to the change in momentum of the object on which it acts.

175. (A) Momentum is conserved:

$$mv_o = -\frac{m}{4}(2v_o) + \frac{3mv'}{4}$$

$v' = 2v_o$ to the right

176. (E) The impulse is equal to the area under the force vs. time graph, which is −36 N s from 0 to 3 s, then + 36 N s from 3 s to 6 s, giving a net impulse of zero. Impulse is equal to the change in momentum of the mass, so the change in momentum is also zero.

177. (C) The area under the graph from 0 to 3 s represents the change in momentum of the mass.

$$-36 \text{ N s} = m\Delta v = (2 \text{ kg})v_3$$

$$v_3 = 18 \frac{\text{m}}{\text{s}}$$

178. (A) Since the momentum of the center of mass of the cannon and cannonball is zero before they are fired, the momentum of the center of mass must remain stationary after the cannon is fired.

179. (E) The vector sum of the choices must be equal in magnitude and direction of the given vector. The resultant of answer (E) lies between the vectors shown and in the direction of the original given vector.

180. (C) The boy and the sled collide inelastically.

$$m_B v_B = (m_B + m_S)v'$$

$$(20 \text{ kg})\left(3\frac{\text{m}}{\text{s}}\right) = (20 \text{ kg} + 40 \text{ kg}) \, v'$$

$$v' = 1.0 \frac{\text{m}}{\text{s}}$$

181. (A) Momentum is conserved before and after the boy jumps off the sled:

$$(m_B + m_S)v' = m_s v_s$$

$$(60 \text{ kg})\left(1\frac{m}{s}\right) = (40 \text{ kg})v'_s$$

$$v'_s = 1.5\frac{m}{s}$$

182. (C) The impulse J is the area under the triangle:

$$J = Area = \frac{1}{2}(20 \text{ N})(1 \text{ s}) = 10 \text{ N s}$$

183. (D) The impulse is equal to the change in momentum of the mass:

$$10 \text{ N s} = m_1\left(4\frac{m}{s}\right) - m_1\left(1.5\frac{m}{s}\right)$$

$$m_1 = 4 \text{ kg}$$

184. (E) The speed the 1 kg block was moving just before striking the 1.5 kg block can be found by applying conservation of momentum.

$$m_1 v_1 = (m_1 + m_2)v'$$

$$(1 \text{ kg})v_1 = (1 \text{ kg} + 1.5 \text{ kg})\left(5\frac{m}{s}\right)$$

$$v_1 = 12.5\frac{m}{s}$$

Applying conservation of energy to the top and bottom of the ramp before the collision,

$$m_1 gh = \frac{1}{2}m_1 v_1^2$$

$$h = \frac{v_1^2}{2g} = \frac{\left(12.5\frac{m}{s}\right)^2}{2\left(10\frac{m}{s^2}\right)} = 7.8 \text{ m}$$

185. (C) Momentum is conserved before and after the dart strikes the block:

$$m_1 v_o = (m_1 + m_2)v'$$

$$1v_o = (1+4)v'$$

$$v' = \frac{1}{5}v_o$$

Applying conservation of energy after the collision,

$$(m_1 + m_2)gh = \frac{1}{2}(m_1 + m_2)v'^2$$

$$5mgh = \frac{1}{2}(5m)\left(\frac{1}{5}v_o\right)^2$$

$$v_o = \sqrt{50gh}$$

186. (B) Since there is no friction, or other external forces, the momentum in Figure I is equal to the momentum in Figure III, as if the blocks collided elastically in between.

187. (A) Any time a smaller mass collides with a larger mass in what is essentially an elastic collision between Figure I and Figure III, the smaller block will reverse its direction of motion.

188. (E) The impulse vector **J** is applied perpendicularly to the surface of the ramp (up and to the right) and the velocity rebounds from the surface at the same angle to the normal in which it struck the surface, which causes the velocity vector **v** to be directed to the right.

189. (B) Since the collision with the plane is elastic, the speed with which it rebounds is equal to the speed it strikes the plane. Setting the potential energy at height h equal to the kinetic energy just before or after striking the plane gives

$$mgh = \frac{1}{2}mv^2$$

$$v = \sqrt{2gh}$$

190. (A) The mass of the sand at $t = 4$ s is $60(4s)^2 = 960$ kg. Conservation of momentum after 4 s gives

$$m_o v_o = (m_o + m_s)v'$$

$$(1000 \text{ kg})\left(2\frac{\text{m}}{\text{s}}\right) = (1960 \text{ kg}) \, v'$$

$$v' = 1\frac{\text{m}}{\text{s}}$$

191. (C) Applying conservation of momentum just after the collision gives

$$m_1 v_o = (m_1 + m_2)v'$$

$$(800 \text{ kg})\left(10\frac{\text{m}}{\text{s}}\right) = (800 \text{ kg} + m)\left(\frac{6}{0+1}\right)$$

$$m = 533 \text{ kg}$$

192. (D) The resisting force is proportional to the acceleration of each car during the collision.

$$v = \frac{6}{t+1}$$

$$a = \frac{dv}{dt} = \frac{d}{dt}\left(\frac{6}{t+1}\right) = \frac{d}{dt}[6(t+1)^{-1}] = -6(t+1)^{-2}$$

$$F_{net} = ma = \frac{6m}{(t+1)^2}$$

193. (E) $a = \dfrac{F}{m} = \dfrac{12t^3}{m}$. The velocity as a function of time is the time integral of acceleration:

$$v = \int adt = \int \frac{12t^3}{m} dt = \frac{12t^4}{4m} = \frac{3t^4}{m}$$

194. (B) The net force acting on the dart is equal to the derivative of momentum with respect to time.

$$F_{net} = \frac{dp}{dt} = \frac{d}{dt}(3t^3 + 2t) = 9t^2 + 2 = 9(0.2 \text{ s})^2 + 2 = 2.4 \text{ N}$$

195. (B) The change in momentum of the object is equal to the impulse given to the object, which can be represented by the area under a force vs. time graph.

196. (A) The force acting on an object to change its momentum p is given by the derivative $F = dp/dt$, which represents the slope of a momentum vs. time graph.

197. Momentum is conserved:

$$m_A v_A = (m_A + m_B)v'$$

$$(2 \text{ kg})\left(4\frac{\text{m}}{\text{s}}\right) = (2 \text{ kg} + 4 \text{ kg})\, v'$$

$$v' = \frac{4}{3}\frac{\text{m}}{\text{s}}$$

198. The time of fall is $t = \sqrt{\dfrac{2y}{g}} = \sqrt{\dfrac{2(1.5 \text{ m})}{10 \text{ m/s}^2}} = 0.55 \text{ s}$

$$x = v_x t = \left(\frac{4}{3}\frac{\text{m}}{\text{s}}\right)(0.55 \text{ s}) = 0.7 \text{ m}$$

199. Momentum is conserved:

$$m_A v_A = m_A v'_A + m_B v'_B$$

$$(2 \text{ kg})\left(4\frac{\text{m}}{\text{s}}\right) = (2 \text{ kg})\left(4\frac{\text{m}}{\text{s}}\right) + (4 \text{ kg})v'_B$$

$$v'_B = 2.5\frac{\text{m}}{\text{s}}$$

200. The time of fall is $t = \sqrt{\dfrac{2y}{g}} = \sqrt{\dfrac{2(1.5 \text{ m})}{10 \text{ m/s}^2}} = 0.55 \text{ s}$

$$x = v_x t = \left(2.5\frac{\text{m}}{\text{s}}\right)(0.55 \text{ s}) = 1.4 \text{ m}$$

Chapter 5: Circular and Rotational Motion

201. (D) Since $F_{net} = ma$ and torque $\tau_{net} = I\alpha$, torque is analogous to force.

202. (B) The frictional force acting between the girl and the floor of the merry-go-round serves as the centripetal force directed toward the center of the circle and causing her to move in a circle.

203. (B) The tension in the string provides the centripetal force:

$$F_c = \frac{mv^2}{r}, \text{ so } v = \sqrt{\frac{Fr}{m}} = \sqrt{\frac{(9 \text{ N})(0.5 \text{ m})}{0.5 \text{ kg}}} = 3.0 \frac{m}{s}$$

204. (C) There are only two forces acting on the ball, its weight W, directed downward, and the tension T in the string, which is directed up and at an angle.

205. (C) The horizontal component of the tension provides the centripetal force.

$$T\cos\theta = \frac{mv^2}{R}. \text{ Solving for T gives } T = \frac{mv^2}{R\cos\theta}.$$

206. (B) At the bottom of the circle, the tension T is directed upward and the weight mg is directed downward. The vector sum of these two forces constitute the centripetal force.

$$T - mg = \frac{mv^2}{R}, \text{ so } T = mg + \frac{mv^2}{R}.$$

207. (D) The frictional force f provides the centripetal force.

$$f = \mu mg = \frac{mv^2}{R}, \text{ so } \mu = \frac{v^2}{gR}.$$

208. (B) The weight of the car is directed downward, the normal force is directed perpendicular to the inclined track, and the frictional force keeping the car from sliding up the plane is directed down the plane.

209. (D) Since the normal force and frictional force both have components directed toward the center of the circular track, they both contribute to the centripetal force acting on the car.

210. (D) The fulcrum is the edge of the table. The center of mass of the meter stick is at the 50-cm mark, which is 10 cm to the left of the fulcrum. The 0.05 kg mass should be placed at a certain distance r_m to the right of the fulcrum to just begin to tip. For equilibrium, the clockwise torque should just equal the counterclockwise torque:

$$m_s g r_s = m_m g r_m$$

$$m_s r_s = m_m r_m$$

$$(0.1 \text{ kg})(10 \text{ cm}) = (0.05 \text{ kg}) r_m$$

$$r_m = 20 \text{ cm to the right of the edge of the table}$$

211. (B) For the system to be in equilibrium, clockwise torques must equal counterclockwise torques.

$$m_1 g r_1 = m g r_m + m_2 g r_2$$

$$m_1 r_1 = m r_m + m_2 r_2$$

$$(5 \text{ kg})(50 \text{ cm}) = m(25 \text{ cm}) + (2 \text{ kg})(50 \text{ cm})$$

$$m = 6 \text{ kg}$$

212. (E) The net force acting on the object is the centripetal force.

$$F_{net} = \frac{mv^2}{R} = \frac{(3 \text{ kg}) \left(2 \dfrac{\text{m}}{\text{s}} \right)^2}{3 \text{ m}} = 4 \text{ N}$$

213. (B) The angular momentum $L = mvr = (3 \text{ kg}) \left(2 \dfrac{\text{m}}{\text{s}} \right) (3 \text{ m}) = 12 \dfrac{\text{kg m}^2}{\text{s}}$.

214. (B) The component of the force that acts perpendicular to the rod is $F \cos \theta$, so the torque acting on the rod is $FR \cos \theta$.

215. (E) The angular acceleration $\alpha = \dfrac{\tau}{I} = \dfrac{FR \cos \theta}{I}$.

216. (A) The ballet dancer is reducing her radius of rotation by pulling her arms inward. Her angular momentum $I\omega$ is constant, since decreasing her radius increases her speed proportionally, but she does work by pulling her arms in, so her kinetic energy is not constant, but increases.

217. (E) The angular acceleration of the ball is equal to the second derivative of the angle θ with respect to time.

$$\omega = \frac{d\theta}{dt} = \frac{d}{dt}(4t^2 + 3t) = 8t + 3$$

$$\alpha = \frac{d\omega}{dt} = \frac{d}{dt}(8t + 3) = 8\frac{\text{rad}}{\text{s}^2}$$

218. (B) The linear speed of the ball is equal to the product of the angular speed and radius at $t = 3$ s.

$$\omega = 8t + 3$$

$$v = \omega r = [8(3\text{ s}) + 3](2\text{ m}) = 54\text{ m/s}$$

219. (D) The tension in the string pulls up on the left end of the rod causing a clockwise rotation about Point P. The reaction force pushes the rod away from the wall as well as providing a component of force directed upward to counteract the torque produced by the tension in the rope.

220. (A) The angular momentum of the particle corresponds to the perpendicular distance from the origin, which is x_o.

$$L = mvx_o$$

221. (A) The rotational inertia of the system is $\sum I = \frac{1}{12}mL^2 + m\left(\frac{1}{2}L\right)^2 = \frac{1}{3}mL^2$.

222. (E) The net torque is $4mgL - 3mgL = mgL$ clockwise.

223. (D) The angular acceleration $\alpha = \frac{\tau}{I} = \frac{mgL}{4mL^2 + 9mL^2} = \frac{g}{13L}$.

224. (A) The total kinetic energy of the hoop is converted to potential energy at the height h.

$$\frac{1}{2}mv^2 + \frac{1}{2}I\omega^2 = mgh$$

$$\frac{1}{2}mv^2 + \frac{1}{2}(mR^2)\left(\frac{v}{R}\right)^2 = mgh$$

$$h = \frac{v^2}{g}$$

225. (E) The centripetal acceleration of the ball at point Y is directed upward, toward the center of the circle, but the acceleration of the ball at point Z has two components: one in the direction of the tension in the string (toward the center) and the other straight downward due to gravity. The resultant acceleration of the ball at point Z is therefore down and to the right.

226. (C) The net torque acting on the rod is Fr. The torque produced in diagram (C) is $2F\cos 60° r = Fr$.

227. (C) At point C, the bottom of the circle, the force the bug has to supply to hang on has to be the greatest, since the tension is pulling away from the ball and bug. At the top of the circle, the bug would have the ball to rest on, and wouldn't have to apply as much force to stay on the ball.

228. (E) At point C, the bug has to hang on with a force equal to both the centripetal force and its own weight.

$$F_c = F_{\text{bug}} - mg = m\omega^2 r$$

$$F_{\text{bug}} = m\omega^2 r + mg$$

229. (E) The angle through 2 revolutions is $\theta = 2(2\pi \text{ rad}) = 4\pi$ rad. Using a kinematic equation relating angular speed to angular acceleration,

$$\omega = \sqrt{2\alpha\theta} = \sqrt{2\alpha(4\pi)} = \sqrt{8\pi\alpha}$$

230. (E) The ratio of angular momenta is $\dfrac{L_1}{L_2} = \dfrac{I_1\omega_1}{I_2\omega_2} = \dfrac{\frac{1}{2}mr^2\omega}{\frac{1}{2}(2m)(4r)^2\omega} = \dfrac{8}{1}$.

231. (A) The rotational inertia is greatest when the most mass is the farthest distance away, which places the pivot point at the left end of the rod.

232. (D) The net torque is $Fr + Fr - 2F(3r) = -4Fr$. Since the question asks only for the magnitude of the torque, the net torque can be written as $4Fr$.

233. (A) The skater moves with constant velocity from A to B and C to D, indicated by zero acceleration on the first and third sections of the graph. On the curves from B to C and D to A, there is a centripetal force acting on the skater causing a constant centripetal acceleration in these intervals, indicated by the horizontal lines in the second and fourth intervals of the graph.

234. (C) The net torque is $\tau = I\alpha = \dfrac{I(\omega_f - \omega_o)}{\Delta t}$.

235. (D) The power is related to the torque by $P = \tau\omega = \dfrac{I\omega_o}{\Delta t}\omega_o = \dfrac{I\omega_o^2}{\Delta t}$.

236. (D) Angular momentum is conserved as the radius is shortened, so $mv_1\, r_1 = m\, v_2\, (1/4\, r_1)$ gives $v_2 = 4\, v_1$.

237. (A) Since the ball rolls without slipping, the relationship between velocity and angular velocity is $v = r\omega$.

238. (C) Since the ball is rolling and slipping, the speed v of the ball must be less than $r\omega$, since the ball will rotate with an angular speed less than ω. In this case, the speed of the ball cannot be calculated without knowing more about the kinetic friction acting on the ball.

239. (D) The frictional force must be equal and opposite to the weight of the rider for the rider to remain stationary on the wall. If the friction were less than the weight, the rider would slide downward.

240. (E) Since the apparatus is floating freely in space, there are no external forces to change the momentum or angular momentum. Kinetic energy is not conserved because the clay is deformed in the inelastic collision.

241. (D) Angular momentum is conserved during the collision.

$$mvL = I\omega$$

$$\omega = \frac{mvL}{I}$$

242. (A) The weight is directed downward, the normal force is directed perpendicular to the plane, and the friction force causes a clockwise torque on the sphere by pulling the contact point up the plane.

243. (B) Using conservation of energy,

$$mgh = \frac{1}{2}mv^2 + \frac{1}{2}I\omega^2 = \frac{1}{2}mv^2 + \frac{1}{2}\left(\frac{2}{3}mR^2\right)\left(\frac{v}{R}\right)^2$$

Solving for the speed v gives $v = \sqrt{\dfrac{6gh}{5}}$.

244. (C) The angular speeds of the disks are not equal, but the linear velocity of each disk is the same. So, $v = r_1\omega_1 = 2r_2\omega_2$, giving $\omega_2 = \frac{1}{2}\,\omega$.

245. (B) The change in potential energy of the stick is equal to the kinetic energy of the stick at the bottom of the swing. The change in height of the center of mass of the stick is $L/2$. So the change in potential energy as the stick swings is $\Delta U = mg\left(\dfrac{L}{2}\right)$, which is equal to the kinetic energy at the bottom of the swing.

$$mg\left(\frac{L}{2}\right) = \frac{1}{2}I\omega^2$$

$$\omega = \sqrt{\frac{mgL}{I}}$$

246. The torque on the disk is caused by the tension T in the string.

$$\tau = TR = I\alpha = I\left(\frac{a}{R}\right). \text{ So the tension is } T = \frac{Ia}{R^2}.$$

247. The rate of change of the angular speed is the angular acceleration.

$$\alpha = \frac{\tau}{I} = \frac{TR}{I}$$

248. The angular momentum is $L = I\omega = (2 \text{ kgm}^2)\left(2\dfrac{\text{rad}}{\text{s}}\right) = 4\dfrac{\text{kgm}^2}{\text{s}}$

249. The angular acceleration is the rate of change of angular speed with respect to time.

$$\alpha = \frac{\Delta\omega}{\Delta t} = \frac{2\dfrac{\text{rad}}{\text{s}}}{2 \text{ s}} = 1\frac{\text{rad}}{\text{s}^2}$$

250. The rotational kinetic energy is $K = \dfrac{1}{2}I\omega^2 = \dfrac{1}{2}(2 \text{ kgm}^2)\left(2\dfrac{\text{rad}}{\text{s}}\right)^2 = 4 \text{ J.}$

Chapter 6: Oscillations and Gravitation

251. (E) Mass does not affect the period of a pendulum. Only the length and acceleration due to gravity affect the period.

252. (D) Hooke's law states that the force applied by the spring is proportional to the stretch distance, $F = -kx$. The potential energy of the spring is maximum at the amplitude, and the kinetic energy of the mass on the spring is maximum at the equilibrium. Conservation of energy dictates that PE at the amplitude is equal to the KE at the equilibrium position.

253. (A) At the amplitude, the spring force equals the weight of the mass. Setting the spring force equal to the weight of the mass gives

$$kA = mg$$

$$A = \frac{mg}{k} = \frac{(1 \text{ kg})\left(10 \frac{\text{m}}{\text{s}^2}\right)}{20 \frac{\text{N}}{\text{m}}} = \frac{1}{2} \text{ m}$$

254. (B) The period of oscillation is given by

$$T = 2\pi\sqrt{\frac{m}{k}} = 2\pi\sqrt{\frac{1}{20}} \text{ s}$$

255. (B) A freely falling object falls the first 5 m in 1 s by the equation $y = \frac{1}{2} gt^2$. The ball will repeatedly bounce back up to 5 m in perfectly elastic collisions with the floor.

256. (A) The mass begins at the amplitude (stretch distance x is maximum) at a time when the kinetic energy is zero and the potential energy is a maximum. The kinetic energy is maximum and the potential energy is zero when the stretch distance x is zero (equilibrium position). The object's stretch distance is zero at $t = 1$ and 3, so the kinetic energy is maximum at those points. The cycle continues, showing a curved graph for kinetic energy, due to the object's acceleration throughout the cycle.

257. (C) The mass begins at the amplitude (stretch distance x is maximum) at a time when the kinetic energy is zero and the potential energy is a maximum. The kinetic energy is maximum and the potential energy is zero when the stretch distance x is zero (equilibrium position). The object's stretch distance is maximum at $t = 0$, 2, and 4, so the potential energy is maximum at those points. The cycle continues, showing a curved graph for potential energy, due to the object's acceleration throughout the cycle.

258. (D) The period T is related to the angular frequency by the equation $\omega = \dfrac{2\pi}{T} = 4$, so the period is $T = \dfrac{2\pi}{\omega} = \dfrac{2\pi}{4} = \dfrac{\pi}{2}$ s.

259. (B) The equation for the frequency f of a pendulum is $f = \dfrac{1}{2\pi}\sqrt{\dfrac{g}{L}}$, so decreasing the length to $\frac{1}{4}L$ increases the frequency by $2f$.

260. (B) Two springs connected in parallel doubles the spring constant to $2k$, which doubles the frequency and halves the period.

261. (C) A higher spring constant k indicates a stiffer spring, that is, for a higher k, it takes more force to stretch it than a spring of lower k. So the frequency of a spring of higher k will be higher than one of a lower k. Also, we could consider the equation for the frequency of an object in simple harmonic motion, $= \dfrac{1}{2\pi}\sqrt{\dfrac{k}{m}}$, showing that a higher k gives a higher frequency.

262. (A) The acceleration of the mass is caused by the spring force:

$$F_s = ma$$

$$-kx = m\frac{d^2x}{dt^2}$$

$$\frac{d^2x}{dt^2} = \frac{-k}{m}x$$

263. (C) The position of the mass as a function of time is given by the equation $x = A\cos(\omega t)$, where $\omega = \sqrt{\dfrac{k}{m}}$ giving $x = x_o \cos\sqrt{\dfrac{k}{m}}t$.

264. (B) The angular frequency ω is related to the spring constant and mass by $\omega = \sqrt{\dfrac{k}{m}}$, where k/m = 4. So $\omega = \sqrt{\dfrac{4}{1}} = 2\dfrac{\text{rad}}{\text{s}}$.

265. (A) Based on the equation for the angular frequency in the previous question, the mass must be 1 kg.

266. (D) The equation for the period of oscillation is given by

$$T = 2\pi\sqrt{\frac{m}{k}} = 2\pi\sqrt{\frac{1}{4}} = \pi \text{ s}$$

267. (B) According to the equation for the period of a pendulum, $T = 2\pi\sqrt{\dfrac{L}{g}}$, to decrease the period by ½, we must increase the acceleration due to gravity to $4\,g$.

268. (C) The potential energy at the amplitude x_o is equal to the maximum kinetic energy $K = \dfrac{1}{2}mv_{max}^2$. Setting the maximum potential energy equal to the maximum kinetic energy,

$$\frac{1}{2}kx_o^2 = \frac{1}{2}mv_{max}^2 \text{ gives } v_{max} = \sqrt{\frac{k}{m}}x_o$$

269. (E) Conservation of momentum gives the speed of the two masses after they collide and stick together:

$$m_1v_1 = (m_1 + m_2)v'$$

$$m_Bv_B = (m_B + m_S)v'$$

$$(1 \text{ kg})\left(4\frac{m}{s}\right) = (1 \text{ kg} + 1 \text{ kg})\,v'$$

$$v' = 2.0\,\frac{m}{s}$$

Conservation of energy gives us the spring constant by setting the kinetic energy of the blocks equal to the potential energy in the spring.

$$\frac{1}{2}kx_o^2 = \frac{1}{2}mv^2$$

$$\frac{1}{2}k(0.5 \text{ m})^2 = \frac{1}{2}(2 \text{ kg})\left(2\frac{m}{s}\right)^2$$

$$k = 32\frac{N}{m}$$

270. (B) To find the speed of the block when it leaves the table, we set the potential energy of the compressed spring equal to the kinetic energy of the block:

$$\frac{1}{2}kx_o^2 = \frac{1}{2}mv^2$$

$$v = \sqrt{\frac{kx^2}{m}} = \sqrt{\frac{\left(5\frac{N}{m}\right)(1\text{ m})^2}{0.5\text{ kg}}} = 3.2\frac{m}{s}.$$ This velocity is the horizontal velocity

of the block as it leaves the table. The time for the block to fall to the floor is =

$$\sqrt{\frac{2y}{g}} = \sqrt{\frac{2(1.5\text{ m})}{10\text{ m/s}^2}} = 0.55\text{ s}.$$ The block lands a distance x from the base of the table:

$$x = v_x t = \left(3.2\frac{m}{s}\right)(0.55\text{ s}) = 1.7\text{ m}$$

271. (C) The kinetic energy is constant before the collision as well as after the collision, but is converted to potential energy in the spring during the collision, momentarily reducing the kinetic energy of the system.

272. (E) The equation for the acceleration due to gravity is $g = \dfrac{GM}{R^2}$, so the acceleration due to gravity at $4R$ is $g = \dfrac{GM}{(4R)^2} = \dfrac{g}{16}$.

273. (D) With the planet being ¼ M and ½ R, the acceleration becomes

$$g = \frac{G\left(\dfrac{1}{4}M\right)}{\left(\dfrac{1}{2}R\right)^2} = g = 10\frac{m}{s^2}.$$

274. (B) The angular momentum is constant throughout the entire orbit, but the kinetic energy decreases as the satellite moves farther away from the Earth. This is due to the fact that potential energy increases from A to B, and the total energy remains constant.

275. (D) For g to be the same for each planet, the radius of the planet of mass $9M$ would have to be $= \dfrac{G(9M)}{(3R)^2}$, or $3R$.

276. (A) The acceleration due to gravity for Planet Y is $g = \dfrac{GM}{(3R)^2} = \dfrac{1}{9}g$, which means the acceleration for Planet X is 9 times the acceleration for Planet Y.

277. (A) The equation for the speed of a satellite orbiting at a radius R is $v = \sqrt{\dfrac{GM}{R}}$.

For the speed to double to $2v$, the radius would have to decrease to $2v = \sqrt{\dfrac{GM}{\left(\dfrac{1}{4}R\right)}}$,

or ¼ R.

278. (E) Newton's 3rd law of motion states that for every action force there is an equal and opposite reaction force. The two objects apply equal and opposite forces to each other, but the resulting acceleration of each is not the same.

279. (C) Newton's law of universal gravitation is given by $F = \dfrac{Gm_1 m_2}{R^2}$. Doubling one mass and tripling the distance between them gives $F = \dfrac{G(2m_1)m_2}{(3R)^2} = \dfrac{2}{9}$.

280. (C) The speed of a planet in a circular orbit is $v = \sqrt{\dfrac{GM}{R}} = \dfrac{2\pi R}{T}$, where T is

the period of orbit. Rearranging for the period gives $T = \sqrt{\dfrac{4\pi^2 R^3}{GM}}$.

281. (B) Angular momentum is conserved as the satellite orbits.

$$mv_a a = mv_b b$$

$$v_a = \frac{bv}{a}$$

282. (C) Gravitational potential energy is high and negative when the two masses are far apart, and low and negative when they are close together. The potential energy depends on $1/r$, so the graph curves upward.

283. (C) The two masses accelerate toward each other due to the increasing gravitational force between them as they approach, giving answer (C) as the correct U vs. t graph.

284. (B) Since the gravitational force acting on the satellite increases as it travels closer to the Earth, the acceleration also increases.

285. (B) Since the speed of the satellite is slightly too large to stay in a circular orbit, the satellite is at its closest approach to the planet at its original point. The other side of the planet becomes the farthest point, where it is moving at its slowest speed.

286. (C) Since the speed of the satellite is slightly too small to stay in a circular orbit, the satellite is at its farthest approach to the planet at its original point. The other side of the planet becomes the closest point, where it is moving at its fastest speed.

287. (E) The equation for the gravitational force between the stars is equal to the equation for centripetal force:

$$F_G = \frac{GMM}{R^2} = \frac{Mv^2}{\frac{1}{2}R}$$

$$v = \sqrt{\frac{GM}{2R}}$$

288. (A) Since the satellite is still at the same radius r for the moment, its potential energy has not changed when it changes its speed. Therefore the work done to change the satellite's orbit comes from the change in kinetic energy.

289. (D) A satellite is held in orbit by both the (negative) potential energy and (positive) kinetic energy of the satellite, and the sum of the two is the total energy of the satellite, which is zero. The potential energy at a particular orbit cannot change, so increasing the kinetic energy to exceed the potential energy will give the satellite enough energy to escape.

290. (A) Since momentum is conserved, the total momentum after the collision is equal to the total momentum before the collision.

$$2mv - mv = mv$$

clockwise, that is, in the direction of the larger mass.

291. (E) Conservation of momentum gives

$$2mv - mv = 3mv'$$

$$v' = \frac{v}{3}$$

292. (C) The potential energy of the ball at the top of the tunnel is equal to the kinetic energy of the ball at the center of the planet.

$$\frac{GmM}{R} = \frac{1}{2}mv^2$$

$$v = \sqrt{\frac{2GM}{R}}$$

293. (E) The ball will accelerate toward the center, pass the center with maximum speed, then slow down as it approaches the other side of the planet, rising to its original height. Then it will fall back down the tunnel and repeat the process. The ball oscillates about the center of the planet, like a mass on a spring.

294. The potential energy is equal to the kinetic energy when the potential energy reaches half its original value.

$$\frac{1}{2}kx^2 = \frac{1}{2}\left(\frac{1}{2}kA^2\right)$$

$$x = \frac{A}{\sqrt{2}}$$

295. According to Hooke's law, $F = kx = kA$. The spring force is equal to the weight of the mass.

$$F = kx = kA = ma$$

$$a = \frac{kA}{m}$$

296. The mass oscillates once in 2 s, so the frequency is ½ Hz.

297. The amplitude of oscillation is 2 m. The equation for the position of the mass as a function of time is $x = A\cos(\omega t)$.

$$x = 2\cos(2\pi\, f t) = 2\cos(\pi t)$$

The speed is $v = \dfrac{dx}{dt} = \dfrac{d}{dt}[2\cos(\pi t)] = 2\pi\sin(\pi t)$

298. The period of the stars is the same.

$$T_1 = T_2$$

$$\sqrt{\frac{4\pi^2 r^3}{GM_2}} = \sqrt{\frac{4\pi^2 (2r)^3}{GM_1}}$$

Solving for the ratio of the two masses gives

$$\frac{M_1}{M_2} = 8$$

299. The acceleration due to gravity for each star is

$$a_1 = \frac{GM}{r^2} \text{ and } a_2 = \frac{GM}{(2r)^2}, \text{ giving } \frac{a_1}{a_2} = 4.$$

300. Both stars make one revolution in the same amount of time, so $T_1 = T_2$.

Chapter 7: Electric Force, Field, Potential, Gauss's Law

301. (B) Any charge placed on a spherical conducting surface will spread out evenly around the sphere. A conductor allows the charges to move freely on the surface, and the charges repel each other until they reach equilibrium on the surface.

302. (A) All of the negative charges are on the outside of the sphere, and thus the electric field is zero inside the sphere.

303. (C) The charges will distribute themselves so that the entire surface is at the same potential, otherwise, the charges would move farther based on the difference in potential. Since potential depends on both charge and distance, this would cause charges to bunch up on the narrow portions of the conductor and spread out more on the larger portions of the conductor.

304. (C) The charges will distribute themselves so that the entire surface is at the same potential, otherwise, the charges would move farther based on the difference in potential. Since potential depends on both charge and distance, this would cause charges to bunch up on the narrow portions of the conductor and spread out more on the larger portions of the conductor to create an equipotential surface on the entire conductor.

305. (E) The total charge on the spheres is $-2\,\mu C$. When a wire connects the spheres, the charge redistributes itself so each sphere has $-1\,\mu C$ of charge. The original force between the spheres was $F = \dfrac{K(+1\mu C)(-3\mu C)}{r^2}$ and is now $F = \dfrac{K(-1\mu C)(-1\mu C)}{r^2}$, so the new force between the spheres is $\dfrac{1}{3}F$, and is repulsive, since both charges are negative.

306. (A) By symmetry, both the electric field and electric potential are zero at the center of the sphere, since the distance from each charge is the same to the center of the square, and there are two positive charges and two negative charges at the corners.

307. (B) For the electric field to point upward (positive to negative), there would need to be positive charges on the bottom of the square and negative charges on the top.

308. (C) The charges $+2Q$ and $+Q$ will apply a force down and to the right and to the right, respectively, giving a net field directed down and to the right.

309. (D) Since there is no charge inside the sphere, the electric field is zero everywhere inside the sphere. Then the electric field decreases with $1/r^2$ outside the sphere.

310. (A) Since there is no charge inside the sphere, the electric potential is equal to the potential at the surface of the sphere and remains constant everywhere inside the sphere. Then the electric potential decreases with $1/r$ outside the sphere.

311. (B) The electric field is linearly related to distance from the center of the sphere, $E = Cr$, then decreases with $1/r^2$ outside the sphere.

312. (C) Since the electric potential is proportional to the integral of the electric field with respect to distance r, the potential increases with r^2 inside the sphere, and decreases with $1/r$ outside the sphere.

313. (E) The charge enclosed in a Gaussian sphere of radius r inside the sphere is

$$Q = \int_0^r \rho \, dV = \int_0^r \beta r (4\pi r^2) \, dr = \beta(4\pi) \int_0^r r^3 \, dr = \beta \pi r^4$$

Using Gauss's law,

$$\int E \, dA = \frac{Q_{enc}}{\varepsilon_o}$$

$$E(4\pi r^2) = \frac{\beta \pi r^4}{\varepsilon_o}$$

$$E = \frac{\beta r^2}{4\varepsilon_o}$$

314. (A) The electric potential at the surface of the sphere of radius R can be found by integrating the electric field inside the sphere.

$$V = \int E \, dr = \int \frac{\beta r^2}{4\varepsilon_o} \, dr = \frac{\beta R^3}{4\varepsilon_o}$$

315. (E) Whether the positive charge is moved from A to B or from B to A, the work done is zero, since the whatever energy is gained on the first half the path is lost on the second half of the path. The energy of the positive charge is the same at either of the corners.

316. (B) the electric field will apply a torque and a downward net force on the rod since the larger charge will experience a greater counterclockwise torque and the larger charge will also produce a downward force, causing the rod and charges to accelerate downward.

317. (A) The positive charge in the center will draw the negative charges in the outside conductor to the inside surface of the sphere.

318. (A) When the grounding wire is connected to the outer sphere, more electrons will come up from the ground, since they are attracted to the positive charge in the center, making the outer sphere negatively charged.

319. (D) The electric field inside the sphere of radius a is zero, since there is no enclosed charge in the sphere. The electric field between a and b encloses a charge of $+2Q$ and decreases with $1/r^2$ outside the smaller sphere. Then the electric field outside the sphere encloses a net charge of $+Q$, and decreases with $1/r^2$ outside the sphere.

320. (A) The electric potential is constant inside the smaller sphere and is equal to the potential at the surface of the smaller sphere. Then the electric potential decreases with $1/r$ outside the smaller sphere, and again decreases with $1/r$ outside the sphere.

321. (A) The charges will distribute themselves so that the entire surface is at the same potential, otherwise, the charges would move farther based on the difference in potential. Since potential depends on both charge and distance, this would cause charges to bunch up on the narrow portions of the conductor and spread out more on the larger portions of the conductor to create an equipotential surface on the entire conductor.

322. (C) The electric field can be found by taking the negative derivative of the potential function with respect to r.

$$E = -\frac{dV}{dr} = -\frac{d}{dr}(ar^{-1}) = ar^{-2}$$

323. (D) The work done in moving a charge in an electric field is

$$W = qV = q(Ed) = (4\ \mu C)\left(4000\frac{N}{C}\right)(0.2\ m) = 3200\ \mu J$$

324. (E) The downward force acting on the droplet is its weight

$$mg = (3.2 \; x \; 10^{-7} \, \text{kg}) \left(10 \frac{\text{m}}{\text{s}^2} \right) = 3.2 \; x \; 10^{-6} \, \text{N}.$$

The upward force on the droplet applied by the electric field is

$$qE = (8 \; x \; 10^{-9} \, \text{C}) \left(200 \frac{\text{N}}{\text{C}} \right) = 1.6 \; x \; 10^{-6} \, \text{N}.$$

The downward force is greater than the upward force, so the droplet will accelerate downward.

325. (A) The two spheres carry the same charge, but are not at the same potential, since they are different sizes. The smaller sphere will have the greater surface potential since the charges are closer to each other. Current will flow from the smaller sphere at higher potential to the larger sphere at lower potential.

326. (E) All of the charge on the ring is the same distance from the point on the axis. The distance from any charge on the ring to the point on the axis is the hypotenuse r of the right triangle, and is given by the Pythagorean theorem,

$$r = \sqrt{R^2 + 9d^2}$$

The potential at the point on the axis is then $V = \dfrac{kQ}{r} = \dfrac{kQ}{\sqrt{R^2 + 9d^2}}$.

327. (A) Along the axis, the electric field to the left of the ring is practically zero far away, then increases negatively until it reaches a maximum, then decreases to zero at the center of the ring. Then the electric field becomes positive just to the right of the ring, and repeats the pattern in reverse.

328. (E) Gauss's law states that the electric flux $\int E \cdot dA$ is proportional to the charge enclosed in a closed surface. If the net charge in a closed surface is zero, the flux through the surface is zero, even though the electric field passing through that surface may not be zero.

329. (A) If an electric field is caused by a charge located outside a closed surface, electric field lines would pass through the surface, but the flux into the surface would equal the flux out of the surface, so the net flux would be zero.

330. (B) Electric potential depends on the type of charge (positive or negative) and how far away they are. Electric potential is the work per unit charge done to move a charge through an electric field. Potential is a scalar quantity, and does not depend on direction.

331. (E) The electric field outside of the smaller sphere is $E = \dfrac{kQ}{R^2}$. For the same charge Q on both spheres, the electric field outside of the sphere of radius $4R$ is $E = \dfrac{kQ}{(4R)^2} = E = \dfrac{kQ}{16R^2}$, or 1/16 of the electric field due to the smaller sphere.

332. (E) The electric potential outside of the smaller sphere is $V = \dfrac{kQ}{R}$. For the same charge Q on both spheres, the electric potential outside of the sphere of radius $4R$ is $= \dfrac{kQ}{4R}$, or 1/4 of the electric potential due to the smaller sphere.

333. (C) Electric field lines are always perpendicular to equipotential lines and are directed from higher potential to lower potential.

334. (A) Electric field lines are defined as pointing in the direction a positive charge would move in that field, from higher potential (more positive) to lower potential (more negative).

335. (B) Since the electric field is constant between the plates, the potential decreases at a constant rate as a charge moves from top to bottom. The equipotential lines would be horizontal and evenly spaced, much like a hiker descending down a mountain with a constant slope.

336. (B) Electric field is determined by applying Gauss's law in this case by integrating the flux integral from zero to a to find the electric field inside the sphere, then again outside the sphere to find the electric field at $r > a$. The electric field outside the sphere is the sum of these two integrals.

337. (D) Once you've determined the electric field both inside and outside the sphere, the electric potential inside the sphere is determined by beginning far away from the sphere and integrating the electric field function outside the sphere from infinity to a, then integrating the electric field function inside the sphere from a to x_1. The electric potential at x_1 is the sum of these two integrals.

338. (C) Bringing the positively charged rod near the knob of the electroscope will cause the negative charges in the electroscope to rise to the top and the positive charges in the electroscope to be repelled and go to the leaves. When the student touches the knob with her finger, the positive charges now have a way of escape, and they are drained into the ground, or equivalently, negative charges are brought up from the ground, and the electroscope is now negatively charged.

339. (A) Since the electric field is greater when it exits the cube compared to when it entered the cube, there must be charge enclosed in the cube adding to the electric field as it passes through.

340. (D) According to Gauss's law, the electric flux exiting the cube is due to the charge enclosed in the cube.

$$EA = \frac{q_{enc}}{\varepsilon_o}$$

$$q_{enc} = \varepsilon_o EA = \varepsilon_o (ba^2)(a^2) = \varepsilon_o ba^4$$

341. (E) Since the charge on the larger cylinder is on the inside surface of the cylinder, there is no electric field outside the larger cylinder. Equivalently, the net charge in a Gaussian cylinder around the outside of the cylinders is zero, so the electric field on the outside is zero.

342. (A) Applying Gauss's law between the cylinders gives

$$EA = \frac{q_{enc}}{\varepsilon_o}$$

$$E(2\pi r_2 L) = \frac{Q}{\varepsilon_o}$$

$$E = \frac{Q}{2\pi \varepsilon_o r_2 L}$$

343. (B) Gauss's law is most convenient to use when the charges are arranged symmetrically, such as on a sphere or cylinder.

344. (C) Gauss's law can be derived from the inverse square law $(1/r^2)$, such as the electric force between electric charges, the gravitational force between masses, and the magnetic force.

345. According to Coulomb's law, $F_E = \frac{Kq_1 q_2}{r^2}$, to increase the force to $4F$, the distance between the charges would have to be halved by moving q_1 to $-\frac{1}{2} r$.

346. The electric field would be zero halfway between the equal charges, at $-r$.

347. The electric potential due to a point charge is $V = \sum \frac{kq}{r}$. The potential is the greatest when the point is nearest the most charge, which would be $-r$.

348. The magnitude of the electric field is greatest at point A because the equipotential lines are closer together, indicating a sharper change in electric potential over a smaller distance.

349. The potential difference between points C and D is 10 V, and we can assume that the electric field is relatively constant between the points.

$$E = \frac{V}{d} = \frac{10 \text{ V}}{0.02 \text{ m}} = 500 \frac{\text{V}}{\text{m}}$$

350. The work done in moving a charge through an electric field is

$$W = q\Delta V = (+5.0 \ \mu C)(10 \text{ V}) = +50 \ \mu J$$

Chapter 8: Electric Circuits, Capacitors, Dielectrics

351. (E) The resistance between a and b for circuits 1 and 5 is 2 Ω.

352. (C) Since the two resistors on that branch are equal, they will each have the same voltage across them. The total resistance of the parallel arrangement is $\frac{1}{2\Omega} + \frac{1}{4\Omega} = \frac{3}{4\Omega}$ giving $R_p = \frac{4}{3\Omega}$. The total resistance in the circuit is $R_t = 2\Omega + \frac{4}{3\Omega} = \frac{10}{3\Omega} \Omega$. The parallel voltage is 4/10 of the total voltage, or $\frac{4}{10}(12 \ V) = 4.8$ V. The voltage across the 2 Ω resistor in the right branch is half of this voltage, giving 2.4 V.

353. (B) The voltage across the resistor in the left branch is 4.8 V. The ammeter will read the current as $I = \frac{4.8 \text{ V}}{2\Omega} = 2.4 \text{ A}$.

354. (B) Adding another resistor in parallel decreases the resistance in the circuit, so the current and the reading on the ammeter would increase when another resistor is added in parallel.

355. (A) The emf ε is the slope of the graph of power vs. current, or

$$\varepsilon = \frac{\Delta P}{\Delta I} = \frac{20 \text{ W}}{4 \text{ A}} = 5 \text{ V}$$

356. (C) When the power is 10 W, the current is 2 A. The resistance is

$$R = \frac{P}{I^2} = \frac{10 \text{ W}}{(2 \text{ A})^2} = 2.5\Omega$$

357. (D) The equation for the resistance of a conductor is $R = \frac{\rho L}{A}$, where ρ is resistivity, L is the length of the conductor, and A is the area through which the current passes. Since all of the conductors are the same length and resistivity, the conductor with the smallest area has the highest resistance.

358. (B) The resistance of the two 2-Ω resistors in parallel is 1 Ω. Since 1 A of current is passing through the 2 Ω resistor on the far right, the current through the other 2 Ω resistor must also be 1 A, giving a total current in the circuit of 2 A. According to Ohm's law,

$$R = \frac{V}{I}$$

$$3\Omega + 1\Omega + r = \frac{12 \text{ V}}{2.0 \text{ A}}$$

$$r = 2\Omega$$

359. (D) Charge is related to current by $q = \int_0^2 I\, dt = \int_0^2 4t^3\, dt = t^4 \big]_0^2 = 16$ C.

360. (B) A voltmeter across the battery and its internal resistance would read $6 \text{ V} - Ir = 6 \text{ V} - (1 \text{ A})(2\Omega) = 4$ V.

361. (D) The arrangement that dissipates the most power is related to the equation $P = \frac{V^2}{R}$. For answer (D), this equation gives the most power, 12 W.

362. (C) Since 2 A of current is entering point a and 1 A is leaving point a, there must be 1 A of current passing through the middle branch and through the 3 Ω resistor. So a voltmeter connected across a and b would read $6 \text{ V} + (1 \text{ A})(3\Omega) = 9$ V.

363. (B) Power is high when resistance is low, and drops off with 1/R with constant emf.

364. (A) The arrangement which dissipates the most power is related to the equation $P = \frac{V^2}{R}$. For answer (A), this equation gives a power of 9 W.

365. (A) Bulb 1 will burn the brightest, since it is in a position for the total current to pass through it. The other bulbs only get part of the total current.

366. (C) Bulbs 2 and 3 will not change their brightness, since bulb 4 was connected in parallel to them. Bulbs 2 and 3 still have the same voltage applied across them.

367. (C) Circuit I will not discharge its charge when the battery is removed because it is an open circuit and will retain its charge. Circuit II is still a complete circuit when the battery is removed and will discharge through the resistor.

368. (E) The equation for the capacitance of parallel plates is $C = \dfrac{\varepsilon_o A}{d}$. Changing the quantities as described gives $C = \dfrac{\varepsilon_o (4A)}{\left(\dfrac{1}{2}d\right)} = 8\ C$.

369. (C) Charge, capacitance, and voltage are related by $V = \dfrac{q}{C}$. Setting the voltage across each capacitor equal to each other gives $\dfrac{q_o}{C_o} = \dfrac{q_2}{2C_o}$ gives $\dfrac{q_2}{q_o} = 2$.

370. (A) Since the 8 μF capacitors are in parallel, their capacitances can be added to yield 16 μF. Now we have three capacitors in series:

$$\frac{1}{C_t} = \frac{1}{2\,\mu F} + \frac{1}{16\,\mu F} + \frac{1}{4\,\mu F},\ \text{giving } C_t = 7/4\ \mu F$$

371. (C) The voltage across the 2 μF capacitor is $\left(\dfrac{2}{22}\right)(120\ \text{V}) = 10.9\ \text{V}$. So, the charge on the 2 μF capacitor is $q = CV = (2\ \mu F)(10.9\ \text{V}) = 22\ \mu C$.

372. (A) Current is the flow of charge, and any charge entering a junction must exit that junction. This is a statement of conservation of charge.

373. (D) Since $E = \dfrac{V}{d}$, we now have $E = \dfrac{V}{2d}$, giving half the electric field.

374. (D) The energy stored in the capacitor is $U = \dfrac{1}{2}CV^2 = \dfrac{1}{2}(10\ \mu F)(12\ \text{V})^2 =$ 720 μJ.

375. (D) When the switch is closed, current flows freely through the uncharged capacitor, so the current begins high. As the capacitor charges, it resists the flow of current, and the current decreases exponentially.

376. (D) The graph for the voltage across the resistor will match the graph for the current through the resistor, as in the explanation for the previous question.

377. (B) The voltage across the capacitor begins at zero since it is uncharged. As current decreases in the circuit due to the charging of the capacitor, the voltage across the charged capacitor rises exponentially in the opposite direction of the battery.

378. (E) Capacitors in parallel can be added: $C_t = 10\ \mu F + 10\ \mu F + 10\ \mu F = 30\ \mu F$.

379. (E) The total capacitance in series is given by $\dfrac{1}{C_t} = \dfrac{1}{9\ \mu F} + \dfrac{1}{9\ \mu F} + \dfrac{1}{9\ \mu F} = \dfrac{3}{9\ \mu F}$, or $C_t = 3\ \mu F$. Since the capacitors are in series, they each receive the same charge, which is equal to the total charge in the circuit: $q = CV = (3\ \mu F)(9\ V) = 27\ \mu C$.

380. (E) Since the capacitors are connected in series, each capacitor will have 2 V across it. The energy stored in one of the capacitors is $U = \dfrac{1}{2}CV^2 = \dfrac{1}{2}(6\ \mu F)(2\ V)^2 = 12\ \mu J$.

381. (D) Filling a capacitor with a dielectric increases the capacitance of the capacitor, allowing it to store more charge.

382. (B) Placing another resistor in parallel will decrease the total resistance and increase the current through the circuit, increasing the rate at which the capacitor charges.

383. (B) The maximum current through the resistor is given by Ohm's law. Using the maximum voltage from the battery gives $I = \dfrac{\varepsilon}{R}$.

384. (D) The current starts at zero and increases rapidly as the capacitor begins to charge. The current decreases to zero as the capacitor charges, and when the switch is connected to b, the capacitor discharges, with the current dropping off exponentially.

385. (C) Gauss's law states that $EA = \dfrac{q_{enc}}{\varepsilon_o}$. The charge enclosed can be written as CV, where $V = Ed$. Rearranging gives the equation for capacitance, $C = \dfrac{\varepsilon_o A}{d}$.

386. (C) A parallel-plate capacitor with a dielectric is given by

$$C = \frac{\kappa \varepsilon_o A}{d} = \frac{4\varepsilon_o A}{\frac{1}{2}d} = 8 \text{ C.}$$

387. (A) Gauss's law states that

$$\int E\,dA = \frac{Q_{enc}}{\varepsilon_o}. \text{ Solving for } E:$$

$$E(4\pi r^2) = \frac{Q}{\varepsilon_o} \text{ gives } E = \frac{Q}{4\pi\varepsilon_o r^2}$$

388. (B) They are connected in parallel because the positive top half is connected to the positive bottom half, and the negative top half is connected to the negative bottom half.

389. (C) Since the capacitors are connected in parallel, their capacitances can be added:

$$C_t = \frac{1}{2}C_o + \frac{1}{2}(3C_o) = 2C_o$$

390. (C) Applying Gauss's law between the cylinders gives

$$EA = \frac{q_{enc}}{\varepsilon_o}$$

$$E(2\pi rL) = \frac{Q}{\varepsilon_o}$$

$$E = \frac{Q}{2\pi\varepsilon_o rL}$$

391. (B) They are connected in parallel because the positive larger right-side third is connected to the positive left-side two-thirds, and the negative right-side third is connected to the negative left-side two-thirds.

392. (D) Since the capacitors are connected in parallel, their capacitances can be added:

$$C_t = \frac{2}{3}C_o + \frac{1}{3}(3C_o) = \frac{5}{3}C_o$$

393. (C) When a dielectric is inserted between the plates, a charge is induced inside the dielectric at the tip and the bottom. The induced charge is opposite to the charge on the plates, so they create an electric field opposite to the original electric field between the plates, thus decreasing the net electric field between the plates.

394. The total voltage in the circuit is $6\ V - 3\ V = 3\ V$, since they face opposite directions. Using Ohm's law, $3\ V = (2\ A)(0.2\,\Omega + 0.1\,\Omega + 1.0\,\Omega + R)$, giving $R = 0.2\ \Omega$.

395. Taking the top half of the loop, the voltmeter will read $-3V - (2\ A)(0.2\,\Omega) - (2\ A)(0.1\,\Omega) = -5.4\ V$, or $5.4\ V$, depending on how the voltmeter is connected across a and b.

396. The power dissipated through the $0.1\,\Omega$ resistor is $P = I^2 R = (2\ A)^2(0.1\Omega) = 0.4\ W$. The energy is given by the product of power and time, $E = Pt = (0.4\ W)(30\ s) = 12\ J$.

397. The maximum charge occurs when $t = 0$, leaving $q_{max} = 6\ C$.

398. The charge and current are related by $I = \dfrac{dq}{dt} = \dfrac{d}{dt}\left(6e^{\frac{-t}{4}}\right) = -\dfrac{3}{2}e^{\frac{-t}{4}}$.

399. The number 4 is in the place of the product RC in the general equation for the current produced by a discharging capacitor. The product RC has units of time.

400. The product RC has units of Ω, $F = V/A$, $C/V = C/C/s = $ seconds.

Chapter 9: Magnetic Fields and Forces

401. (D) The magnetic field around the wire at a radius r is given by Ampere's law, $B = \dfrac{\mu_o I}{2\pi r}$, directed out of the page by the right-hand rule.

402. (C) The magnetic field produced by a current flowing through a wire is proportional to $\dfrac{I}{r}$. The magnetic field produced by each wire is $\dfrac{2I}{r}$ and $\dfrac{4I}{2r}$, giving equal magnetic fields.

403. (A) By the right-hand rule applied to each wire, one of the wires produces a magnetic field directed out of the page, and the other produces a magnetic field into the page, giving a net magnetic field of zero.

404. (C) By Newton's 3rd law, the wires exert equal and opposite forces on each other.

405. (B) The magnetic fields produced by opposite currents exert an attractive force on each other.

406. (A) By the right-hand rule, the force on the top of the loop is downward and the force on the bottom of the loop is upward, creating a clockwise torque on the loop and a clockwise rotation.

407. (D) The current through the spring coil creates a magnetic field that interacts with the magnetic field due to the magnet in which the coil rests. The coil experiences a force and a torque, turning proportionally to the current and rotating to make the needle move the proper distance on the meter.

408. (A) Since the currents are in opposite directions, the magnetic fields produced are in the same direction, causing the loops to repel.

409. (E) Since the magnetic force between current-carrying wires depends on the product of the currents, twice the current in each loop will produce four times the force between them.

410. (C) By the right-hand rule, the magnetic field produced by the current in the loop curls to the left on the outside of the loop and to the right through the center of the loop.

411. (C) By the right-hand rule, thumb in the direction of the velocity, fingers in the direction of the magnetic field (into the page), and the force comes out of the palm, up to the top of the page.

412. (D) The current in the loop at the top will experience an upward force by the right-hand rule. The current at the bottom of the loop will experience a downward force. Similarly the current in the 3:00 and 9:00 positions will contribute to the expansion of the loop.

413. (A) Each wire creates an equal and opposite magnetic field at point P, giving a net magnetic field of zero.

414. (E) Both currents create magnetic fields with components to the right, giving a net magnetic field at point N to the right.

415. (C) Using the left-hand rule, since the charge is negative, the force is up to the top of the page.

416. (B) The magnetic force on the electron becomes a centripetal force, causing it to travel in a circular path.

417. (E) The magnetic force is always perpendicular to the velocity of the electron, and therefore cannot change its kinetic energy.

418. (C) By the right-hand rule, the thumb is pointed out of the page and the palm faces up and to the left, giving a magnetic field in the direction of your fingers down and to the right.

419. (C) Since the particle enters the magnetic field at an angle, it moves in a circular path while also moving forward, creating a spiral-shaped path.

420. (D) The magnetic field due to wire 1 is $B_1 = \dfrac{\mu_o I}{2\pi d}$, and the magnetic field due to wire 2 is $B_1 = \dfrac{\mu_o I}{2\pi(2d)}$. Both magnetic fields are in the same direction by the right-hand rule, so the sum of the magnetic fields is $\dfrac{3}{2}B_1$.

421. (C) The magnetic force is given by $F = qvB = (2 \times 10^{-6}\ \text{C})\left(2 \times 10^6\ \dfrac{\text{m}}{\text{s}}\right)$ $(0.2\ \text{T}) = 0.8\ \text{N}$ to the right by the right-hand rule.

422. (D) Since the positive charge experiences a magnetic force to the right, the electric field must be established to apply an electric force on the charge to the left. Thus the electric field must be directed to the left.

423. (A) Using the left-hand rule for the negative charge, the magnetic force acting on the charge is directed down toward the bottom of the page. Thus the electric field, which points in the direction a positive charge would experience a force, must be also directed downward.

424. (B) For the charge to follow a straight-line path in the electric and magnetic fields, the net force acting on the charge must be zero. Setting the electric force equal to the magnetic force,

$$F_E = F_B$$

$$qE = qvB$$

$$E = vB = \left(8 \times 10^6\ \dfrac{\text{m}}{\text{s}}\right)(0.5\ \text{T}) = 4 \times 10^6\ \dfrac{\text{N}}{\text{C}}$$

425. (A) If you follow a positive charge from the top of the sheet to the bottom, it will experience a force to the right by the right-hand rule. Thus, point X becomes positive and has a higher potential than point Y. This is called the Hall effect.

426. (C) Ampere's law states that $\int B \cdot dl = \mu_o I_{enc}$, giving $B(2\pi r) = \mu_o I$.

427. (D) Using Ampere's law, the equation for the magnetic field as a function of distance r from the wire is $\dfrac{\mu_o I}{2\pi r}$, so the magnetic field varies inversely with distance from the wire, giving answer (D).

428. (A) In a perfect solenoid, all of the magnetic field produced by the current is inside the solenoid, so the magnetic field outside the solenoid is zero.

429. (D) Using the right-hand rule, the direction of the magnetic field inside the solenoid is found by curling your fingers around in the direction of the current and the magnetic field points in the direction of your thumb.

430. (B) Since the only segment in the area where there is a magnetic field is a to b, the integral from a to b is the best choice.

431. (E) The magnetic force becomes the centripetal force acting on the charge:

$$F_B = F_C$$

$$qvB = \frac{mv^2}{r}$$

$$\frac{q}{m} = \frac{v}{rB}$$

432. (A) Since the magnetic force is perpendicular to the velocity of the charge, the magnetic force cannot do any work on the charge or change its kinetic energy.

433. (C) According to Ampere's law, the radius r and magnetic field B are inversely related, giving graph (C).

434. (D) The current is the charge per unit time, $I = \dfrac{Q}{T}$.

435. (E) Since the rotation of the charges (current) is clockwise, the magnetic field inside the loop is to the right by the right-hand rule.

436. (D) The magnetic field anywhere on the axis of the ring is to the left by the right-hand rule.

437. (D) Current density is defined as the current per unit area, $J = \dfrac{I}{A} = \dfrac{I}{ab}$.

438. (B) The best symmetry for this situation calls for a rectangular loop for Ampere's law.

439. (B) Using the right-hand rule, put the thumb in the direction of the current (outward) and the fingers curl around to point to the left at point X and to the right at point Y.

440. (D) Using the right-hand rule, put the thumb in the direction of the current (outward) and the fingers curl around to point up and to the left at point M.

441. (E) Using the right-hand rule, put the thumb in the direction of the current (outward) and the fingers curl around to point to the right at point N.

442. (A) Since the two currents are equal and in opposite directions, the net enclosed current is zero and the net magnetic field produced at point P is zero.

443. (E) The magnetic field inside the cylinder of radius a is linear with respect to distance r from the center of the cylinder, then falls off with $1/r$ between a and b, then eventually drops to zero outside the larger cylinder, since the currents are in opposite directions.

444. (E) For any device to register a magnetic field, there has to be relative velocity between the device and the moving charge, in this case a compass. If the compass is moving with the charge, there is no relative velocity, and the compass will not deflect.

445. For the region outside the cylinder, the magnetic field produced is the same as if the cylinder were simply a current-carrying wire. Ampere's law then gives $B = \dfrac{\mu_o I}{2\pi r}$.

446. Applying Ampere's law at a distance r from the center of the cylinder gives $\int \boldsymbol{B} \cdot \boldsymbol{dl} = \mu_o I_{enc}$ where I_{enc} is related to the ratio of current passing through the area enclosed by r and the area enclosed by a:

$$B(2\pi r) = \mu_o I \left(\frac{\pi r^2}{\pi a^2} \right), \text{ giving } B = \frac{\mu_o I r}{2\pi a^2}$$

447. The magnetic field inside the conductor is proportional to the distance r from the center, so the first segment of the graph is linear. Then the magnetic field drops off with $1/r$ outside the conductor.

448. The electric potential difference ΔV is related to the work done on the charge, which is equal to the change in kinetic energy of the charge.

$$W = \Delta KE$$

$$q\Delta V = \frac{1}{2}mv^2$$

$$\Delta V = \frac{mv^2}{2q}$$

449. Since the electron enters the magnetic field perpendicularly, we can use the left-hand rule to determine that the force on the charge is up to the top of the page, and causes the electron to travel in a circular path labeled A.

450. The magnetic force becomes the centripetal force acting on the charge:

$$F_B = F_C$$

$$qvB = \frac{mv^2}{r}$$

$$r = \frac{mv}{qB}$$

Chapter 10: Electromagnetic Induction, Inductance, and Maxwell's Equations

451. (D) According to Faraday's law of induction, the magnetic flux must be changing for a current to be induced in a loop. Either the magnetic field can be changing or the area through which it passes can be changing.

452. (D) According to Ohm's law, $I = \dfrac{\varepsilon}{R}$. The induced emf in the loop is $\varepsilon = \dfrac{-\Delta\Phi}{\Delta t} = \dfrac{-B\Delta A}{\Delta t} = \dfrac{-BL\Delta w}{\Delta t} = BLv$. The current is then $I = \dfrac{\varepsilon}{R} = \dfrac{BLv}{R}$.

453. (D) Since the flux is decreasing through the loop as the loop exits the magnetic field, the induced current in the loop will reinforce the magnetic flux through the loop by creating a current that produces an outward magnetic flux through the loop. Thus, the current must be counterclockwise in the loop according to the right-hand rule.

454. (C) The magnetic flux must change through the loop, and in this situation, the magnetic field is moving downward, which does not change the flux through the loop.

455. (B) The change in magnetic flux through the loop is $\Delta\Phi = \Delta BA = B\Delta A = (0.3 \text{ T})(0.4 \text{ m}^2) = 0.12 \text{ T m}^2$.

456. (A) The induced emf is $\varepsilon = \dfrac{-\Delta\Phi}{\Delta t} = \dfrac{0.12 \text{ T m}^2}{0.2 \text{ s}} = 0.006 \text{ V}$.

457. (E) For the flux through the smaller loop to change, the area of the loop has to be decreased. This cannot be accomplished by rotating it around the x-axis.

458. (C) The magnetic flux through the loop is increasing into the loop. By Lenz's law, current will be induced in the wire to oppose the change that produced it. A counterclockwise current will oppose the change in magnetic flux through the loop by the right-hand rule.

459. (D) As the bar falls, its speed increases. The induced emf is related to the speed of the bar by the equation $\varepsilon = BLv$. The speed increases (relatively) linearly as it falls. So, the induced emf in the rod is proportional to the falling velocity, and increases linearly with the speed.

460. (C) The emf produced in the loop is $\varepsilon = \dfrac{-d\Phi}{dt} = A\dfrac{-dB}{dt} = ab\dfrac{-dB}{dt}$. Dropping

the negative sign, the rate of change in magnetic field is $\dfrac{dB}{dt} = \dfrac{\varepsilon}{ab} = \dfrac{IR}{ab}$.

461. (B) The flux through the closed loop is increasing inward, since the area through which the flux passes is increasing, so the induced current in the bar is to the right to oppose the change in flux by Lenz's law.

462. (C) The magnetic force acting on the bar is $F = ILB = \dfrac{BLv}{R}LB = \dfrac{B^2L^2v}{R}$.

463. (A) As the front of the loop enters the magnetic field, the flux begins to increase through the loop. Since the speed is constant, the change in flux area increases at a constant rate from zero to w. The flux is constant while the entire loop is in the magnetic field, then the flux decreases constantly as the loop exits the magnetic field. The flux is zero after the loop completely exits the field.

464. (A) By Lenz's law, the magnetic force produced by the induced current will oppose the motion of the loop, somewhat like friction.

465. (C) The magnitude of the induced emf in the loop is $\varepsilon = \dfrac{\Delta\Phi}{\Delta t} = \dfrac{A\Delta B}{\Delta t} = \dfrac{(0.2 \text{ m})^2(0.1 \text{ T})}{4\text{s}} = 0.001$ V. The induced current is then $I = \dfrac{\varepsilon}{R} = \dfrac{0.001 \text{ V}}{0.5\Omega} = 0.002$ A.

466. (A) As the north pole of the magnet is pushed into the loop, the magnetic flux is increasing into the loop, producing an induced current into the page that will oppose the change in flux. Then as the magnet is pulled out of the loop, the induced current will produce a magnetic flux that opposes the decrease in flux, and reverse its direction, coming out of the page.

467. (C) The component of the weight directed down the incline is $mg\sin\theta$, and is the force causing the acceleration of the bar.

$$F_{net} = mg\sin\theta = ma$$

$$a = g\sin\theta = \left(10\frac{\text{m}}{\text{s}^2}\right)(\sin 30°) = 5\frac{\text{m}}{\text{s}^2}$$

468. (C) A component of gravity points down the incline, and an opposing magnetic force is produced by the induced current in the bar as it moves down the rails.

469. (E) When the bar reaches its final speed, it is no longer accelerating, and the magnetic force is equal to $mg\sin\theta$.

$$mg\sin\theta = ILB$$

$$I = \frac{mg\sin\theta}{LB} = \frac{(0.2 \text{ kg})\left(10\frac{\text{m}}{\text{s}^2}\right)(\sin 30°)}{(0.3 \text{ m})(0.3 \text{ T})} = 10 \text{ A}$$

470. (A) The magnetic flux through the loop is $\Phi = BA\cos\theta = (0.3 \text{ T})(0.3 \text{ m})(0.6 \text{ m})\cos 30° = 0.0078 \text{ T m}^2$.

471. (D) The rate of change of magnetic flux is $\dfrac{-d\Phi}{dt} = A\dfrac{dB}{dt} = s^2\dfrac{dB}{dt} = s^2\dfrac{d}{dt}(k+Ct) = s^2 C$.

472. (D) Ohm's law states that $I = \dfrac{\varepsilon}{R}$ and the magnitude of the induced emf is $\varepsilon = \dfrac{d\Phi}{dt} = s^2 C$. The current is $I = \dfrac{s^2 C}{R}$.

473. (E) By the right-hand rule, the current (thumb) on the near side is to the right, the magnetic field (fingers) is down to the bottom of the page, and the force (palm) on the wire is into the page away from you.

474. (D) The induced emf in the loop is related to the change in flux by the equation $\varepsilon = \dfrac{d\Phi}{dt} = A\dfrac{dB}{dt} = \pi r^2\dfrac{dB}{dt} = k\pi r^2 t^{\frac{3}{2}}$. Solving for the rate of change of magnetic field gives $\dfrac{dB}{dt} = kt^{\frac{3}{2}}$.

Separating variables and integrating the magnetic field gives

$$B = \int dB = \int kt^{\frac{3}{2}} dt = \frac{2}{3}kt^{\frac{5}{2}}.$$

475. (A) For the loop to remain suspended in equilibrium, the upward magnetic force must equal the weight downward.

$$F_B = F_C$$

$$IaB = mg$$

$$I = \frac{mg}{aB}$$

476. (B) The current is induced in the wire because the magnetic flux is changing.

$$\varepsilon = \frac{d\Phi}{dt} = A\frac{dB}{dt} = \pi r^2 \frac{dB}{dt} = \pi r^2 \frac{d}{dt}(B_o - kt) = -k\pi r^2$$

Using Ohm's law,

$$I = \frac{\varepsilon}{R} = \frac{k\pi r^2}{R}$$

477. (B) The electric field at the radius r can be found by integrating the emf around the loop:

$$\varepsilon = \int E dl$$

$$k\pi r^2 = E(2\pi r)$$

$$E = \frac{kb}{2}$$

478. (C) The magnetic flux as a function of time is

$$\Phi = BA = A(4e^{-2t}) = 4Ae^{-2t}$$

479. (C) The induced emf can be found by

$$\varepsilon = \frac{-d\Phi}{dt} = -A\frac{dB}{dt} = -A\frac{d}{dt}(4e^{-2t}) = 8Ae^{-2t}$$

By Ohm's law,

$$I = \frac{\varepsilon}{R} = \frac{8Ae^{-2t}}{R}$$

480. (E) Energy is the product of power and time, or in this case $\int_0^\infty P dt = \int_0^\infty I^2 R dt$.

481. (A) When $bt > 1$, the current in the wire is positive and decreasing, producing a flux through the loop that is decreasing. The magnetic field due to the current-carrying wire is out of the page by the right-hand rule.

482. (D) The flux integral $\int B \cdot dA$ begins at y and goes to $y + s$, since this is the region of space occupied by the loop.

483. (A) When the switch is closed, the inductor first greatly opposes the voltage from the battery by Lenz's law, so the voltage is low across the resistor. As current begins to flow, the inductor opposes the battery voltage with less back emf until the current in the circuit is constant, and the voltage across the resistor is equal to the emf provided by the battery. When the current is steady, the inductor does not oppose the emf from the battery and current flows freely through it.

484. (C) According to Lenz's law, the inductor will oppose a *change* in current. Since the *change* in current is high when the switch is first closed, the back emf from the inductor is high to oppose the change. The back emf in the inductor then decreases as the current in the circuit becomes more steady (less change). Eventually, the voltage across the inductor is zero when the current is steady.

485. (C) Inductance L is measured in Henrys, and resistance is measured in ohms. So, $\dfrac{H}{\Omega} = \dfrac{\frac{V}{A/s}}{\Omega} = \dfrac{A\Omega}{\Omega A/s} = \text{seconds}$.

486. (C) The back emf due to the changing current is found by

$$\varepsilon_L = -L\frac{dI}{dt} = -L\frac{d}{dt}(3t^2) = -L(6t) = -(0.5\ \text{H})[6(2\ \text{s})] = -6\ \text{V}$$

487. (A) According to the loop rule, the sum of the voltages around the circuit is zero. The voltage ε rises through the battery, then drops across the resistor $(-IR)$, then drops through the inductor $\left(-L\dfrac{dI}{dt}\right)$.

488. (D) After a long time, the inductor stores magnetic energy, so when the switch is connected to b, the emf across the inductor causes current to continue to flow through the two resistors $(2R)$. Using the loop rule, the sum of the voltage drops around the circuit and gives $-2IR - L\dfrac{dI}{dt} = 0$.

489. (C) This is called an LC circuit, and the energy oscillates between the capacitor and the inductor. Sometimes this circuit is called an oscillating circuit.

490. (B) The flux of magnetic field through a closed surface is zero, since any field lines exiting the closed surface from the north pole of the magnet will reenter the closed surface into the south pole. The magnetic flux would not be zero if there was only one pole enclosed in the surface.

491. (A) Gauss's law for electrostatics states that the flux of electric field through a closed surface is caused by the charge enclosed in the surface.

492. (C) Ampere's law states that the magnetic field integrated around a closed path is related to the current enclosed in that path.

493. (D) Faraday's law of induction relates the induced emf ε to changing magnetic flux $d\Phi/dt$. Integrating the electric field along a path gives the emf ε and the rate of change of magnetic flux.

494. (E) Gauss's law can be applied to gravity, since the gravitation force and acceleration are inverse square laws. We can say that the flux of the gravitational field g is related to the mass enclosed in a closed surface.

495. Since the flux is increasing outward, the current induced in the loop will create a change in flux that opposes the increasing magnetic flux, producing a current that is clockwise by the right-hand rule.

496. Ohm's law states that $I = \dfrac{\varepsilon}{R} = \dfrac{A\dfrac{dB}{dt}}{R} = \dfrac{\pi a^2}{R}\dfrac{dB}{dt}$.

497. The induced current of the loop at radius $2a$ is $I = \dfrac{\varepsilon}{R} = \dfrac{A\dfrac{dB}{dt}}{R} = \dfrac{\pi (2a)^2}{R}\dfrac{dB}{dt}$.

498. When the switch is connected at a, the back emf is highest, and is equal and opposite to the battery emf, 6V.

499. After a long time, the current is steady and the inductor provides no back emf. The current is given by Ohm's law:

$$I = \frac{\varepsilon}{R} = \frac{6\text{ V}}{2\Omega} = 3\text{A}$$

500. When the current is a steady 3 A, the energy stored in the inductor is

$$U = \frac{1}{2}LI^2 = \frac{1}{2}(0.1\text{ H})(3\text{A})^2 = 0.45\text{ J}$$